RANK AND FILE

Rank and File

Hugh Jenkins

CROOM HELM LONDON

©1980 Hugh Jenkins
Croom Helm Ltd, 2-10 St John's Road, London SW11

British Library Cataloguing in Publication Data

Jenkins, Hugh, b. *1908*
  Rank and file.
  1. Putney Labour Party
  I. Title
  329.9'421'66   JN1129.L35P8

  ISBN 0-7099-0331-6
  ISBN 0-1400-8 Pbk

Typeset by Elephant Productions, London SE22
Printed and bound in Great Britain

CONTENTS

RANK AND FILE

To the members of the Putney Labour Party

FOREWORD

Tony Benn

Why do men and women join the Labour Party? What is a local party really like at constituency and branch level? What inspires and what discourages its members? How do they work together and what value do they attach to their efforts? What do they believe in and argue about, and how do they settle the differences that arise? What do they think of the situation now and what are their hopes for the future?

Hugh Jenkins, a member of the Putney Labour Party, its active and respected MP for over 15 momentous years, and a distinguished Arts Minister in Harold Wilson's Government has, through this book, enabled Putney's leading Labour activists to answer those questions for themselves.

In these extended interviews Hugh has given the readers of this book a chance to learn more about the Labour Party, at grass roots level, than they could learn in a lifetime from the mass media. And in his own shrewd prologue and epilogue he has set these stories within a framework of history and analysis.

This is a very good — and a very important — book for the Labour movement, and all who want to understand it. For it is a curious fact that the coverage of Labour Party politics in the newspapers, and on television and radio, concentrates almost exclusively on the role of the parliamentary and National Executive leadership. Constituency parties are ignored except during the week of annual conference when the media dismiss the constituency delegates as unrepresentative extremists who can be safely disregarded and their policies ignored even if they are carried by conference votes.

Part of the reason for this treatment of the constituencies can be explained by the unhealthy concentration upon personality politics; part of it derives from a deep establishment hostility to the fact that the constituency parties are, and have always been, seriously committed to the democratic transformation of Britain towards socialism. Part of the explanation can be traced to the failure of the media to study and report faithfully upon the work of the constituencies and the public ignorance which follows from that neglect.

Here at last is a book which fills that void with real, named, people who comprise the Putney Party and have made it the force it is in serving those who live in the area at local and national level. No constituency is typical and Putney has unique characteristics that identify it clearly as a London party including among its members many people who are well known as individuals for their work.

We learn about the individual background of 40 men and women, and of the experiences that brought them into the Labour Party; and in some cases of actions by a Labour Government which disillusioned them for a time.

We hear from left, right and centre and how they see the issues that have divided them, and why despite it all, they remain so committed to work together.

We also learn a bit about the history of the party, and from Hugh Jenkins himself, of the time when Ray Gunter was chairman of the NEC organisation committee and conducted an enquiry into the Putney Party because it allowed its banner to be carried on the Aldermaston march!

It is no wonder that so many of these rank and file interviews bring out the hopes for more tolerance and for a more collective leadership in the future than that of the 1950s and early 1960s.

After 30 years as a Labour MP I have good reason to know the value of dedicated local parties. They are made up of those who have, in the main, no personal ambitions to corrupt their judgement. Some may seek and win a seat on the Council. A very few may stand for Parliament but the vast majority of them work without any personal recognition because they believe in what they are doing.

As a result their instincts are usually surer than are those at the top in Parliament or government.

Any examination of constituency party resolutions, passed over the years, will establish that beyond dispute; and also reveal that constituency party policy is often a decade ahead of its time — and of the national leadership.

Indeed the conflicts of view between rank and file on the one hand, and the leadership on the other is not usually susceptible to the crude analysis of 'extreme' versus 'moderate'.

It is the difference between the principled stand of the party workers, and the compromises arising from the 'here and now' pressures and temptations of office to which those at the top are subjected.

Nor should that surprise us, for all pressures for democracy, socialism and reform has always, and always will, come from outside the existing power structure and be forced upon it. Understandably the status quo becomes much more tolerable to any group — even

10

Labour leaders — who by virtue of an election victory find themselves pitchforked to the top positions within the status quo; armed with the authority to run it. It is very easy for any Labour Minister, or Labour Committee, to confuse his or her occupancy of the seats of power with the arrival of socialism, for such a muddle between 'Labour in office' and 'socialism in practice' can only be clarified with the help of the rank and file who can be relied upon to perceive the difference between the two without any difficulty. That, of course, is why party democracy is so crucial now. For without it Labour in office can actually hinder the advance of socialism.

The accountability of all elected representatives; the right of the rank and file to determine policy and to monitor its implementation; and the establishment of a collective leadership must be achieved if real progress is to be made.

This book makes all this clear through the experiences and convictions of those whose work and efforts make the Labour Party a real force in British politics.

It was in Putney Church that the historic debates about the future of democracy in Britain took place between the Levellers and the Grandees in Cromwell's army, so it is singularly appropriate that we should now be able to follow the progress of the debate in Putney 330 years later.

Hugh Jenkins was fortunate to represent such people in Parliament, and they were fortunate to have such a representative and, now, to rediscover him in a new capacity as the chronicler of their experiences and their hopes for the future.

PROLOGUE

As Disraeli said, 'Without Party, Parliamentary Government is impossible.' And as Winston Churchill said, some time later, 'We are, more than we know, the creatures of our institutions.'

These two observations by celebrated Tories contain within them the reasons for the continuing conflict which has long existed between the Labour Party in the country and its representatives in Parliament. Parliamentarians know in their hearts that they need the party system, yet their everyday conduct in the Chambers of the two Houses, and the traditions that govern that behaviour, all assume that the party is a thing apart. The institution of Parliament recognises the existence of party grudgingly and the longer a Member remains a part of the institution the stronger is the temptation for him to accept its mores. Indeed it might be said that the common course for a Labour MP is to tread in the footsteps of Herbert Morrison; to start as a socialist and finish up as a parliamentarian.

Relations between party and government are almost as various as there are countries and parties, ranging from such extremes as the Soviet Union, where the outsider finds it difficult to distinguish between government and party, to the United States where the role of the party seems to be to concern itself with electioneering rather than with policy. Other Labour and social-democratic parties appear in most countries to enjoy a rather more influential, if not domineering role, in relation to their representatives in Parliament than is the case here. For example, it is not unusual for the parliamentary Leader to be the choice of the party as a whole and it is also the case that Cabinets as well as Shadow Cabinets are elected by the parliamentary party rather than appointed by its Leader.

In this country, the Labour *parliamentary* party alone elects the Leader. In office, he becomes Prime Minister and appoints the rest of the government, thus establishing the spoils systems and a parliamentary dictatorship in which all are dependent for their office on the whims of a single man. In opposition, the parliamentary party elects not only the Leader but the nucleus of the Shadow Cabinet; the allocation of the Shadow portfolios is, however, still the prerogative of the Leader.

The rank and file party member in the country is excluded from all this. He can move motions on policy at his ward branch and if he is elected as a member of the General Committee of his constituency party he can have a say in determining the membership of the National Executive Committee of the Labour Party but his only line of communication to the parliamentary Labour Party is through his Labour Member if he has one. If he belongs to that half of the country which has no Labour MP most of the time, then the rank and file member of the party has no effective political voice in Parliament.

For many years this was considered to be an appropriate and proper state of affairs. Before 1964 the National Executive of the Labour Party was seldom in disagreement with the parliamentary Labour Party and at Annual Conferences constituency resolutions and selections were consistently voted down by the great trade unions whose leadership during those years was generally on the right of the party. It was not until Annual Conference and the National Executive itself was captured by the left that the party in the country began to think it possible to influence Parliament and government.

As will be seen in the following pages, as late as 1963, the National Executive was firmly on the right of the party and concerned itself not with seeking to influence the parliamentary Labour Party but rather in trying to keep under control the rising power of the left in the constituency parties. In those years most of the full-time party officials were also drawn from the conformist wing of the party and they enthusiastically carried out instructions to root out and suppress elements in the party who were easily seen as 'influenced by Moscow.' In point of fact, the rising left in the constituency parties, like its leaders Aneurin Bevan and Michael Foot, were seldom under Communist influence and many were actively hostile to Stalinism and all its manifestations, but such details have never deflected the right of the party in its determination to keep the party on a gradualist and conformist course.

The roots of this hostility towards the rank and file and the determination to keep the constituency parties firmly in their place stem from the earliest days of the party when the concurrent existence of the Independent Labour Party and the Labour Party itself engendered bitter enmity between the party in government and its supporters in the country which, of course, rose to a peak when Ramsay Macdonald seceded from the party to form a National Government. That great betrayal has left scars on the Labour Party which have never entirely healed.

In recent years clashes between constituency parties and their Members of Parliament have arisen as the result of the Member failing to take due account of party policy and gradually moving

14

towards a more establishment or even Conservative point of view, as in the case of Reg Prentice. There have been cases in the past when Members of strong socialist convictions have found themselves out ahead of their local parties and attempts to get rid of them have been made, not because of their lack of socialist ardour but because of their excess of it; William Warbey and Konni Zilliacus come to mind. In such cases, left or right, it is hard to avoid the view that the Member has failed to maintain close contact with his constituency party. Complaints from MPs that attempts to sack them are being made by small unrepresentative groups (which is what they call the General Committee of their party) would be more convincing if one had ever heard complaints from Members that they were selected by the same small, unrepresentative group. What is good for selection is good for de-selection.

For many years the constituency party representation on the National Executive of the Labour Party has been consistently left wing; what moved the party as a whole in that direction from the sixties onwards was the development of progressive policies and the arrival of less hidebound personalities at the head of the great trade unions; the consequent move to the left changed the balance of power in the Labour Party. Hitherto the trade unions and the parliamentary leadership had combined to crush the constituency parties year after year, but in more recent years the picture has been one of the majority of the trade unions and constituency parties combining together to produce forward-looking policies and a National Executive Committee which saw itself as standing well out ahead of a reluctant and slow-moving parliamentary party.

The position has been complicated by changes in the constituency parties themselves, exemplified by the Putney Party which until 1963 was dominated by a group totally hostile to such organisations as the Campaign for Nuclear Disarmament which was seen as the current equivalent of the Communists of old. This suspicion, in turn, stemmed from the attempts of the Communist Party and of Trotskyist groups over many years to affiliate with, or infiltrate into, the Labour Party. And so men and women who had begun as crusading socialists became defensive and suspicious and saw new ideas and new personalities not as a source of refreshment and reinforcement, but as a challenge and an usurpation.

The strains and stresses which have arisen between parliamentary representatives and constituency parties have not been seen to anything like the same degree at municipal level. The Councillor does not get cut off from his constituency party; on the contrary, he is usually a leading worker in it and he has less temptation to adopt a new way of life, make new friends and move in exalted circles. Even more important, the Local Government Committee where he may meet members of his General Committee, keeps the constituency activist and the Councillor in communication with each other. If they disagree, at least they know what they are disagreeing about. The committee structure of the Council, in which every member of the Council plays some part in an aspect of policy formation and implementation, prevents the sharp separation which occurs in Parliament between government member and back-bencher; it is high time that the Cabinet system of government was re-examined for the present set-up is divisive and inefficient. The Cabinet Minister, or even the Shadow Cabinet member, is removed from the rank and filer, physically, psychologically and emotionally, and what is surprising is not that separation occurs but that occasionally individuals break through the barriers and establish an indentity of purpose in which the whole party is united.

This book has nothing to say about the civil service, which features prominently in my previous volume, *The Culture Gap*. Here we are concerned with the rank and file of the Labour Party but while we are discussing the reasons for the alienation of affection which has too often occurred between MP and constituency party it must be said that differences of view have often emerged after the MP has enjoyed the experience of government. When a Labour Government moves into office the effect is too near that of pouring a warm pink jelly into an old cold mould. The individual minister is suddenly cut off from party contacts and submerged in a flood of private and confidential paper presented with deferential skill. Over a period of time, he will need constant ideological support if he is not to begin to see problems through new eyes; to see the advantages of leaving well alone, to see the difficulties of change and, in doing so, to acquire the beginnings of contempt for those whose views he once shared but now sees as ill-informed and jejune. Fortunately, this only happens to a few but they include people of the most forceful outward character. If ever a minister told me that he was completely in charge of his department, I would know at once that, without realising it, he had been totally dominated by the civil service.

The enquiry now taking place into the organisation of the Labour Party will, I hope, take into consideration the kind of rank and file view to be found in this book. What surprised me was the strong view held over a wide spectrum of opinion that the active party member is, at present, deprived of a proper share in decision-making

16

and that power is over-centralised in the hands of the Prime Minister. I have myself long believed this to be so but I did not know that my view was so generally held.

The leadership of the party, especially in office, has always held the view that its role is to contain the enthusiasms of the more eager socialists in the party's ranks in the effort to retain support of less committed members of the party, of the mass of Labour voters who are not members of the party (and who are assumed to be more conformist than the active member) and of the floating voter.

As against this, the active rank and file, implicitly or explicitly, emphasise the role of leadership in politics, of leadership at the grass roots level and of the vital importance of sustaining the socialist morale of the party by carrying out in office the full socialist policies adopted by the Annual Conference of the party. In this concept the enthusiasm engendered by socialist action is catching and the high morale of such a party would sweep Labour to power and sustain the party in office throughout all vicissitudes.

The Putney experience tends to support the rank and file idea rather than the accepted practice which has dominated Labour Party politics throughout most of its history.

Another way of expressing the differences of view within the Labour Party is to say, as Tony Benn has done, that we are divided between those of us who are concerned to try to make capitalism work humanely and those determined to introduce the new socialist society. It is possible to present this difference as one of time rather than of objective; to say that we all want socialism sometime, but some are more impatient than others. The trouble with this is that as the rank·and file see it, or as most of them seem to see it in my experience and in this book, the leadership of the party has spent much of its effort in government over the years trying to patch up a capitalism which will not work and to sustain an acquisitive society which refuses even to support a welfare state at a reasonable level of human efficiency. Of course, no one argues that parliamentary democracy, which most of us value deeply, could produce a new society overnight even if the Cabinet consisted solely of members of the Tribune group; what is being said is that a Labour Government should make progress towards a more just society and should not be content to stand still let alone walk backwards. The limitations on a minority government are also understood as are the economic realities of life, both national and international, but it is pointed out that Labour with a very comfortable majority in 1966 devoted itself in Parliament to riveting on the shackles of the Economic Community with its commitment to the free capitalist market and the economic theories of Milton Friedman, instead of undertaking any perceptible movement towards the creation of the new democratic socialist society.

What is being sought by the Putney Labour Party and by members of the rank and file of the party throughout the country is a leadership responsive to the aims and ambitions of the party as expressed at its annual conferences and in its policy statements and election manifestos. In its struggle for such a leadership the Putney Party first sought to secure a Member of Parliament, or at any rate, a candidate for Parliament, of its own mind. That struggle began in the early sixties and although the main and most important part of this book consists of the views of 'rank and file' members of the Putney Party, we must begin by setting the scene.

* * *

On 17 April 1963 David Grugeon, then Honorary Secretary of the Putney Labour Party wrote to Sara Barker, National Agent of the Party. 'I understand that an administrative problem has arisen in the consideration of the endorsement of Mr Hugh Jenkins as Prospective Parliamentary Candidate for Putney', he said. It was the last bloody straw.

I was rising 55. Chairman of 'Victory for Socialism' and on the Executive of the Campaign for Nuclear Disarmament, I was correctly seen as belonging to the left of a party which had always been dominated by its right wing. As a result, earlier efforts to become a Member of Parliament, which had never been concentrated or single-minded, had easily been frustrated by the establishment within the party which, in those days, saw its own left as the chief enemy. So I had abandoned hope of getting into Parliament years before, soon after I had been defeated by Robert Carr at Mitcham in 1955. Now I bitterly regretted changing my mind and agreeing to join in the rat race once again. I should never be allowed to get into the House and should not have consented to go forward for selection. I must have been out of my mind for I was perfectly happy as Assistant General Secretary of Equity, Chairman of the Theatres Advisory Council and a Labour member of the London County Council. With all this I could have gone on successfully until retirement. Why bring frustration and grief down on myself yet again?

In his letter David Grugeon went on to explain that in the expectation that my candidature would be endorsed at the National Executive meeting of 14 April, a full programme had been arranged beginning with a public meeting at Wandsworth Town Hall on 30 April. Surely the NEC could endorse a candidate who had been endorsed both in 1950 and in 1955 and let Putney get on with the task of winning the constituency for Labour?

In point of fact Putney had never been won for Labour and as it had been lost once again by over 5,000 votes in 1959, by Dick Taverne, there was little reason to suppose we could break the Tory grip on the constituency.

Sara Barker replied that the candidature had not been before the Organisation Sub-committee and, therefore, although I had been chosen on 6 April, the matter would not reach the National Executive until the end of May. Meanwhile I could not be announced as prospective parliamentary candidate. A warning came from Bill Jones, the Assistant Regional Organiser of the Party. 'Tread warily.' he said, 'or Jenkins may not be endorsed.'

The background of this extraordinary state of affairs was even more bizarre. When my wife and I moved to Putney in 1958 the constituency was firmly in the hands of a small right-wing group. Their choice of Dick Taverne (who later left the Labour Party on the grounds that it was too socialist) as their candidate for the 1959 general election, was typical of their approach to politics. We joined the local party as a matter of course and worked for Taverne without success in the 1959 election.

Marie and I had come from Pimlico. We had moved there in 1954 to be near the House of Commons when I had thought I should win Mitcham, which had been made into a safe Labour seat by the Boundary Commission's decision to take off the Tory area of Wallington. Unhappily, they changed their minds. We had been members of the Westminster Labour Party which had thrown off an attempt by Trotskyists to gain control. While we were there the ruling right wingers had lumped Marie and I in with the Trots because we were not on Hugh Gaitskell's side in his struggle against the Bevanites. I found that when Labour parties to whom I had been recommended as a possible parliamentary candidate wrote to the Westminster Party, they received a negative response. We decided to move out and chose Putney because there was a flat vacant overlooking the river. We still live there.

I fought the 1955 general election in Mitcham against nuclear weapons and founded there the first anti-hydrogen bomb campaign, so by the time we came to Putney our political position was known. We were glad to find *in situ* such fellow nuclear disarmers as Russ and Anne Kerr and it was inevitable that the argument developed within the Putney Labour Party. This was seen by members of the controlling group as an organised attempt to oust them and, in 1962, a dozen nuclear disarmers called at our flat to ask whether I would stand as parliamentary candidate. I immediately refused saying that I was finished with all that and that Anne Kerr, who represented the area on the London County Council, was their obvious choice. They said that Anne was up for Rochester and that with me as candidate the seat could be won. Marie and I both laughed at this and they went away but left behind some election figures. I studied them and when they came back, in spite of Marie's grave doubts I agreed that my name should go forward.

I was so nervous at the Selection Conference that I made the second worst speech I have ever made. The worst was in moving the Suez resolution at the Labour Party Conference of 1956 and as both these dreadful utterances were followed by success it suggests that although the pen may be mightier than the sword, organisation is more effective than speech.

Immediately after the Selection Conference Sara Barker wrote from Transport House to David Grugeon saying that decisions taken by the Putney Party to participate in the Aldermaston March and to take the party banner on the march were 'quite unconstitutional' and 'not in order'. Individual members of the party could participate in the activities of the Campaign for Nuclear Disarmament but party organisations must not give it official support. A number of members of the Putney General Management Committee had written protesting about the majority decision and they had every right to do so. Putney must not act unconstitutionally.

Grugeon replied immediately asking to see evidence of an NEC decision that the party 'must not give official support to the CND'. Sara Barker was unable to produce any such statement and that Easter Putney took its banner on the Aldermaston March, and I helped to carry it part of the way. Members of the party were anxious that I should not do so as they believed that attempts would be made to link the two issues in an endeavour to nullify my adoption. I simply did not believe this but immediately prior to the National Executive meeting which was to consider the matter a story appeared in the *Daily Mail* which was clearly leaked by hostile elements in and around Transport House. Under the heading 'Ban-Bomb clash menaces Labour unity', Keith McDowall reported that at its May meeting the NEC would receive two recommendations which had been moved by Ray Gunter, MP, Chairman of the Organisation Sub-committee. One was that an enquiry be held into the Putney Labour Party, the other that endorsement of my candidature should, meanwhile, be deferred. The story said, quite inaccurately, that I had been the 'main instigator' of the proposal to take the banner on the march. It also reported, correctly this time, that Dick Crossman and Tony Greenwood had protested at the proposal to defer endorsement of my nomination.

When the National Executive met on 22 May the proposal to hold an enquiry into the Putney Party was carried; that to defer my candidature was defeated because people who disagreed with my position on nuclear disarmament nevertheless knew me to be a proper Labour candidate and voted accordingly. Among them was Jim Callaghan.

Meanwhile Putney had proceeded with the public meeting, taking care not to announce me as its chosen prospective candidate but, of course, the local papers picked up the story and splashed it on their front pages. I have always believed that we were helped to win Putney against the odds in 1964 precisely because it became known that the right in the party was trying to upset the local choice. My name came sharply before the electorate long before the election and there was generated in the Putney Labour Party and outside it a powerful conviction that someone Gunter and his like wanted to keep out *must*, somehow or other, be got in.

David Grugeon decided to give up the Hon. Secretaryship, as his work was taking him out of London for a year. Before he did so he issued a statement to the Putney Party in which he recalled that the proposal to take part in the Aldermaston March had come from Thamesfield Ward which had carried it by 21 to 13; that the Young Socialists had suggested that we carry the banner by 22 to 11 and that I took no part in either of these debates. His own actions in the matter had been endorsed by the General Management Committee with only three dissentients and a motion from the Fairfield Ward protesting against the decision about the banner had been lost by 29 to 4. He added that I had secured 38 votes at the Selection Conference and that the man who came second had secured 23. This was exactly the number who had signed the letter to the National Agent which had caused all the trouble.

Sara Barker wrote on 26 June to say that the enquiry into the affairs of the Putney Labour Party would be conducted by Ray Gunter MP, Arthur Skeffington MP and herself. They wished to meet the Officers and Executive Committee of the Putney Party in July at Transport House together with the 23 signatories to the letter.

According to reports which reached me at the time, the meetings at

Transport House reached a pitch of high farce made the more excruciating by the solemnity with which the proceedings were approached by the three inquisitors.

Ray Gunter opened by saying that the enquiry was not solely concerned with the matter of the banner. They were anxious to find the root of the trouble and to eradicate it.

The complaint of the 23 was outlined by Denis Sweaney who had been Hon. Sec. of the party until his resignation in 1961. He said that Putney had been taken over by the Campaign for Nuclear Disarmament. They had become such an effective pressure group that they had a majority on the General Management Committee and no one who was not CND was now considered for any position in the Putney Party. Two members of the party who were considering standing at the Selection Conference had withdrawn because they felt they would have no chance against the group who were determined to get Hugh Jenkins in. Similarly, David Grugeon, a CND member, had been preferred to Frank Reeves for Party Secretary. If the enquiry did not recommend the NEC to expel the CND members, the non-CNDs would withdraw from active membership and leave the party in the hands of nuclear disarmers.

Councillor Loughton said that he was one of those who had withdrawn from the Selection Conference. The party could not have his house for a Committee Room if domination by CND continued. Hugh Jenkins had not said a word against the banner motion. Loughton added that these people operated just like the Communist Party in earlier years.

Mrs Peggy Inman had been told that when Hugh Jenkins had been asked whether he wished to meet Hugh Gaitskell, he had answered, 'Not bloody likely.'

Alderman James said that David Grugeon had been working actively with the Youth Section. These people, including Hugh Jenkins, had not been acting in the true interests of the party for they had failed to oppose the taking of the banner on the Aldermaston March.

Sid Gowlett said that Frank Nodes, an earlier full-time Secretary Agent, had warned him that CND was out to capture Putney. He had seen an article in *John Bull* to this effect.

Brian Easton said that he was opposed to CND but things had been done in a democratic way and this was difficult to challenge. Anti-CND people just stopped being active.

Jean Goehr refuted what the extreme anti-CND people had said. There was a spirit of bitterness abroad. CND people did not always realise the effect they were having on others. They were not a caucus, all the same, They worked together because they knew each other and had the same aims. They dominated the party.

Gunter: 'Did you say, dominated?' Goehr: 'Yes, but they do it democratically.'

Mrs Malleson agreed. She said that when one group dominated, the minority got bitter and vindictive.

Gunter invited Grugeon to reply. He said he was a member of the YS, so why should he not work with it? There was really nothing to reply to.

Skeffington tried to stop Kevin Walsh from speaking but Gunter said he could have a brief reply. He said little and the Chairman of the party, Alf Barton, said that he was not, himself, a CND supporter but everything had been done democratically. The complaint was really that the right, to which he belonged, though he thought of himself as centre, had been in charge of Putney all along and did not like now being ousted from control by this new lot. There was nothing to enquire into.

Stan Chamings said that he was CND but he got on very well with the Chairman and greatly respected him. Mr Leech said there was something wrong. Putney could not be won for Labour by Hugh Jenkins.

I should add here that I was not myself present, nor invited to be present at either of these meetings but happily, the precedent of the original Putney Debates was followed and a verbatim note taken at the time by one of the participants. Unhappily, neither in content nor in form did the later occasion match the noble discussions in the church by Putney Bridge.

However, the outcome was rather different. If Gunter was a latter-day Cromwell, he did not triumph over the Levellers – if the CNDers could aspire to that comparison. The friends of the Labour establishment did not win in Putney and the constituency has never reverted to the tame right-wing control which kept it from offering a real challenge to the Tories for so many years. Several of the 23 became my close friends and fellow workers in the socialist cause, others left the district or gave up active participation in politics; some have died.

All that, however, was in the future. In the summer of 1963 things were very different. The Chief Regional Organiser of the party John Keys, and his Assistant, Bill Jones, were instructed by Transport House to conduct an investigation into the Putney Party on the ground. Bill Jones descended on Putney and had several meetings. He had been instructed to pay special attention to the Young Socialists and after meeting the party officers, asked to see the YS officials who were commanded to have their Minute Book, Attendance Register, Membership Records and Account Books available at a meeting. Some difficulty was experienced in producing these documents and relations between Putney and the regional officers became strained. The books of each ward organisation were also required and as no one knew what the purpose of the exercise was, some of the local voluntary officials showed no enthusiasm to comply. Kevin Walsh took the view that the enquiry should be conducted through the Putney Party officials and he resented direct approaches made to the local ward officers at their homes. Not that this was always successful. The attempt to carry out a party purge without the powers of a police state can be unrewarding. One of the regional officials complained that when he called for some books and documents at an inconvenient time at the house of one stalwart, he was told to 'Sod off' in a quite uncomradely fashion.

On 18 December a letter was received from Miss Barker announcing the verdict of the National Executive.

All the members of the Putney GMC other than the 23 were 'severely censured'. The 23 received the NEC's 'warm appreciation of their courage and loyalty'.

The Young Socialists were disbanded and were to be re-formed under the direction of the Regional Youth Officer.

The first of these decisions was received by the Putney GMC with ribald laughter in which some of the 23 joined and from that moment it became possible for Marie and me to begin to heal the wounds.

Putney had, however, become nationally famous and early in the New Year we decided to cash in by holding a TV Stars Ball. This was a raging success — many of the biggest stars of the day came along — largely owing to the organising flair of Clive Dunn and his wife Cilla Morgan who lived in our block of flats in Putney and were great supporters of our Party. They have remained our close friends ever since. It was a great day. We made nearly £500 profit and began to think that we might really win Putney. We had won 12 of the 15 Putney seats on the Borough Council at the 1962 municipal elections, including one secured by my wife, and the Tories had lost control of the Council. Anne Kerr, a CND member had held her Putney seat on the London County Council in 1961 when other Labour candidates had lost. We took the view that provided we avoided going for the middle of the road and presented ourselves at the full pitch of our socialist beliefs, we had a chance of winning. This conviction was and is against the whole tide of political wisdom inside and outside the Labour Party but the evidence suggests that we were correct and that those who go for the safe centre impress no one. The 'Morrisonian Fallacy' derives from a working-class man's mistaken impression of the salariat. The unstated belief behind this idea is that they sit in the middle; the convinced party member must, therefore, lower his voice so as to present his party as a reasonable half-way house organisation calculated to appeal to any rational individual. In a word, politicians must seek to be all things to all men. The snag about this is that they finish up by being nothing much to anyone and positively repulsive to their own supporters.

The contrary view which has paid off in Putney is that elections are motivated by human energy and that this energy can only be released by conviction. The person offering himself for election should therefore concentrate on those aspects of policy likely to appeal most to his own supporters and least to the opposition. He should not be rude to them but should state propositions which his opponents will find offensive and which will cause them to attack him. Only a politician who is being attacked by the enemy can generate support among his own people. Support in the national newspapers or locally is therefore to be avoided since the press and the media generally are classified by Labour voters as belonging to the establishment. By this means a good turn-out of worker may be assured and since they are the opinion-formers in the community, they will see to it that the non-politicals get to the polls. Organisation can build on this, it cannot create an intention to vote unless it is there, as anyone who has done 'knocking up' knows.

Most post-war elections in Britain have been decided not by those who have voted but by those who have not voted. It has not been a question of persuading the uncommitted middle to go to the polls but of each party getting out the largest number of its own supporters. In post-war England there has been little movement from one party to another and, in the all-important marginals, victory has gone to the party with the highest morale, the largest number of workers, the deepest conviction and therefore, the greatest political energy. Success has come to the party which has turned out the largest percentage of its own supporters on polling day.

These facts, known to all who work in marginal seats, are unknown to the parties as a whole and unaccepted by the party hierarchies because permanent seats of power are not occupied by marginal politicians who, in the nature of the business, are here today and gone tomorrow. Party power lies in the hands of safe seat people who live by a series of propositions by which they regularly drive themselves out of office. The chief of these propositions is the slump to the centre by which the front benches in Parliament, aided by civil servants, make themselves so many pots of poison in the eyes of their traditional workers in the country. Mrs Thatcher won the last General Election because she was nearer to her own party workers than Mr Callaghan was to his own people. Popularity in the opinion polls is no substitute for the drive of the people who do the work; that drive is not on offer to the safe centre person; at best it produces deadlock. Harold Wilson only had a large majority when he was believed to be on the left and Ted Heath lost office when he moved to the middle.

The idea that it is possible to appeal over the head of the committed party worker to the uncommitted is another fallacy, demonstrated by the decline in the total vote which has accompanied the transfer of emphasis at election time from local activities to the party political broadcast on radio and television. The appearance of leading politicians on television is more likely to persuade people *not* to vote, for they are not seen under hostile interrogation, which generates support, but as laying down the law, which is likely to produce apathy or hostility rather than enthusiasm.

Democracy is about exchanging opinions; it is about persuasion and exposition, about asking questions and evaluating answers and this is why the referendum is no good and why the opinion poll is a measurement of what people thought at a certain time and not a guide to how they will act on a certain day.

In Putney in 1963, what was generated was widespread discussion and interest. There were two other factors: the first was my own connection with entertainment personalities, which helped people to see that those they knew as television characters did not hesitate to give public support to this socialist; the second was an imaginative and enthusiastic organisation directed by Ian McGarry. A skinny youth in those days, long-haired and be-jeaned, McGarry was persuaded to abandon his work in a bookshop and become a temporary full-time Agent just for the 1964 general election period. Under his guidance Labour was won for Putney in 1964 and, with a larger majority, in 1966. Amazingly, it was held in 1970 when the Tories won nationally and when safer seats all round fell like ninepins and again when the traditionally safe Labour Fairfield Ward was removed by the Boundary Commission in 1974, rendering the seat once again technically unwinnable by Labour. After the second 1974 general election, McGarry felt that his work in Putney was done. I agreed, for his original appointment had been for a few weeks and if he had not then changed he would have risked being a Labour Party Agent for the rest of his life, since he had no ambition to climb the organisational ladder within the party. He was much too talented for that. He had become Leader of the Wandsworth Borough Council, a role he occupied with great distinction and I was delighted when he became Assistant General Secretary of Equity, filling the position I had vacated a decade earlier after my election as Member for Putney in 1964.

Putney was lost to the Tories in 1979. I had passed my seventieth birthday and had asked myself whether I ought to stand again. In the political climate of the time it was felt that Putney would be difficult to win and most people seemed to think that I would have a better chance of holding the seat than any newcomer. On the other hand the Putney Party believed in re-selection and so did I but as it was not yet party policy, for Putney to have held a selection conference would have been widely misunderstood within Putney and elsewhere. The party held a re-adoption meeting at which I was the only candidate and two members of the General Management Committee voted against the motion to re-adopt. Afterwards they made it clear to me that they were protesting against the failure to hold a conference and that if one had been held I would have been their choice.

We had a good campaign by ordinary standards but it could not match the elan of our earlier achievements. Instead of Ian McGarry organising a single constituency we had Ken Solly doing his best to cover both Putney and Tooting. McGarry took the view that even if he had been here and able to concentrate on Putney we should still have lost, for the Tory maojrity exceeded 2,000 and I am inclined to agree that in the circumstances of 1979 there was no way in which Putney could have been held for Labour. As it was the swing against us was less than in many similar constituencies.

Shortly before the 1979 election my first book, *The Culture Gap* which, among other things, told of my experiences as Minister for the Arts from 1974 to 1976 was published. In the aftermath of the election I decided to write a second book, this time about the people who make up the Putney Labour Party. My idea is to present this remarkably variegated group as the idiosyncratic individuals they are and to do it in their own words.

The order in which the interviews appear is not haphazard. In general, as would be natural, the older members come first and the newer recruits later but this sequence is broken from time to time for various reasons. For example, because he appears in this Prologue, David Grugeon's experiences are placed earlier than might otherwise be the case. Again, Ruth Aylett follows her mother, Pamela Aylett, although she is much younger than others who follow later but whose experience in the Putney Party was after hers. And so on. But broadly the order is chronological.

Wherever possible I have allowed information about members to emerge from the interviews but where necessary I have included a factual introductory note. My questions to interviewees are only included where they are needed to explain a change of direction.

MRS FRANCES WYVER

*Widow of George Wyver, founder member
of the Putney Labour Party after whom
the Party HQ 'George Wyver House'
was named. Age 77.*

George died seven years ago at the age of 96. I was his second wife
and we were married soon after the end of the war when George was
already 70. My own most active period in the Labour Party was in
those post-war years when we raised the money to buy and equip our
old HQ at 168 Upper Richmond Rd. Mrs Ina Chaplin was the Labour
candidate at that time and she was very active in getting money
together to buy the building, or rather to put down a deposit and raise
a mortgage. I was never one for politics myself except to help George
and so it is of him and what he told me that I want to talk, not of
myself.

George was brought up in the union, the workhouse, because both
his parents died when he was a child. He often used to say how cruel
it was to be separated from his sister and how much better things are
today. After much hardship he came to London to seek work in
building and secured it at 4½d an hour as an improver. Eventually he
became a stonemason and a member of their craft union which was
subsequently amalgamated with the other building trade unions.
George settled in Putney because it was a good place to reach different
parts of London from and he was working as a journeyman at the
time taking work where he could find it. When we travelled in London
on a 'bus he would often say, 'I did that window or those steps.' He
worked at Hampton Court for 11 years and on Somerset House for 13
years. He loved Hampton Court. He was on maintenance and he adored
that building.

George wrote what he called a 'Summary of my Life' and it says there
that he joined the Independent Labour Party in 1904 and started a
branch in Wandsworth soon after. He always called members of the
Labour Party 'Comrade' even in private conversation.

George served in the Army in France in the First World War and
afterwards took a leading part in the formation of the trade union
movement in building and in the foundation of the Labour Party in
Putney where he stood for the Borough Council and for the LCC on
the Labour ticket but was not elected. He was very active in the

General Strike in 1926.

It was the Labour victory in 1945 which gave him great pleasure and you will recall his triumphant reception of your victory here in Putney in 1964. But in the period before that he became Secretary of the Premises Committee and was responsible for the building and for seeing that the rents were collected from trade unions who used the rooms for their meetings so that we could pay the mortgage. It was practically a full-time job — no wonder they called it George Wyver House! For years and years he ran whist drives every Saturday night to raise money to pay the mortgage. I made buns for refreshments and Mrs Munn made the coffee. It all helped. The Labour Party and that building were George's life towards the end and he came to the meetings for as long as he could walk. When we won Putney for Labour in 1964 it was what George had worked for all his long life.

I am the son of George Wyver by his first wife and I was born in 1909 here in Putney. Father had us brought up as socialists and we attended the Socialist Sunday School which was held in Felsham Road. The Red Flag and the Internationale were both in the hymnbook we used and I have kept my copy of it. Then there were whist drives and dances to raise money for the party. Among those who came to speak were Edward Whitlock who was an active member of the Putney Party. He was a very keen churchman and I remember that as no work could be done on Sundays their Sunday meals were prepared on Saturdays.

On Sunday mornings George, my father, would speak at an open-air meeting on the tow-path near Putney Bridge and sometimes outside Southfields station doing everything he could to get the socialist message across. We had visiting speakers and I remember a man named Saklatvala who became one of the few Communist Members of Parliament, representing Battersea. Once Ramsay Macdonald came and spoke to us at Brandlehow Road School and later on his son, Malcolm Macdonald. Sometimes my father would engage the Conservatives in debate, taking St Mary's Hall in Hotham Road for the purpose of discussing the evils of capitalism or the advantages of socialism. We attended committee rooms to address envelopes and then off out to deliver leaflets. It was almost a family affair for in those days everyone seemed to know everyone else. In 1928 I became the Treasurer of the Putney Labour Party and in 1930 represented the party at the Annual Conference, at Brighton that year. I remember Arthur Henderson, Ben Tillett, Ernest Bevin and Herbert Morrison among many other famous names.

As early as 1922 my father stood for the old London County Council. He was at the foot of the poll but laid the foundations for later successes. Telling of the hardships of his earlier years with its 14-hour day for 15 shillings a week, George said they would not have been pleased if someone had told them they were living in the 'Good old days'!

JACK EAMES

*Parents came to live in Putney from
Redcar, Yorkshire, when Jack was two.
Now 62, he is an active member of the
National Society of Metal Mechanics and
of the Putney Labour Party. Married with
grown-up children and grandchildren.*

I cycle every morning from my home in Putney to my work at CAV
in Acton. When I was seven years old, one of my Sunday morning jobs
was to catch the ha'penny tram into Battersea to pay my father's
trade union dues. His Branch Secretary at that time was George House
who later became MP for Battersea. That was back in the twenties.
We've lived at various addresses all in the Thamesfield part of Putney
almost all my life and I'm still a GLC tenant. I went to All Saints'
School along here, left at 14 and got a job as an errand boy. Then I
decided I was very ignorant and went to night school which cost me
17s 6d a term. I educated myself a bit and then took up the trade as
a fitter/welder. I've been a member of the Labour Party all my life; it's
the only party as far as I'm concerned and if anyone wanted to stop me
being a member they'd have to kill me first.

I always canvass for the party at elections and attend ward meetings
almost every month but I don't seek office in the party or try to get on
the GMC because I'm too busy in my trade union. This year I attended
the Labour Party Conference for the first time as a delegate from my
union. I'm a Trustee of our union and Vice-President of the London
District Council. I'm also Chairman of the Shop Stewards Committee
at work and our branch is affiliated to the Putney Labour Party. I
spend many evenings on trade union work and I'm really tied up. If
I promise to do a thing I want to do it. I don't want to be an absent
member.

When we were kids we used to deliver Labour Party literature but I
never thought we could win Putney until you did in 1964. That was
wonderful — beautiful. I take a leading part in my trade union but
with the Labour Party I'm content to stay in the background and do
the horse work. We're all in it together. I think I'm a bit of an expert
on the trade union side but when it comes to politics, it's not my cup
of tea, I like to let others who can, do that job and I'll support them.
I'm not very clever.

There's a lot more enthusiasm in the Thamesfield Ward than there was at one time. People are more educated. We knew what we wanted when we were younger but we didn't know how to get it. Nowadays the people who are active are more intelligent but the ordinary people are less intelligent — they rely on others too much. When I go to work and walk along a shop floor of about 2,500 people I get the most childish questions asked me and when you've answered them you're treated like a god, they think 'he's a clever chap' but it's ordinary common-sense stuff that everyone should know. With the passing of poverty, the community life has gone with it. In our days although we were poor we used to go in each others houses and chat among ourselves and have parties; people were more open and friendly and more aware of what was going on around them than they are today. Now they go home and turn on the television and that's the start and finish of life.

My son and his wife also belong to the Labour Party but youngsters today don't realise how hard things were. I used to play football and was quite a good boxer — I earned many a pound for six rounds at the boxing booths. When my father met with an accident we lived for a year, believe it or not, here in Putney, on rotten apples. We'd go round for the windfalls and we had them stewed, baked and in every way. I never had a new pair of trousers when I was a kid, it was always my elder brother's handed down to me. We've come a long way and I'm pleased to see the children getting the education now that we fought for for years. One of the most diabolical things this Tory Government is doing is cutting on education. Perhaps they were beginning to realise that working-class children had more brains than children whose education was paid for by their parents. My son graduated at a university and he told me that it was the people who had been to a public paying school who failed their examinations. Now my son is an accountant and a director of his company. He's done well.

But I don't forget that my father got up at four o'clock one morning and walked right across London to North London where he'd heard a job was starting. There was no job so he walked back again. The next day he went to the Labour Exchange and was disqualified for not signing on the day he walked for the job. He asked them to 'phone up the firm who would confirm that he had applied for the job but they refused. They disqualified him from any benefit for six weeks. That's what it was like under the Tories before the war and that's why I hate the Tories. I hate them. I've no other word to express it.

MRS LUCIE HAUSER

Age 61. Widow. Comfortably off.

I was born in Vienna. My father was a banker and we were very well-to-do. My parents had no particular political affiliation but at the age of about twelve I formed a very close friendship, which continues to this day, with a girl whose family were very active in the Austrian Social Democratic Party, the equivalent of the Labour Party. I was an almost daily visitor and politics were always under discussion. I listened avidly, became very interested and was quite soon committed and convinced of the need for social reform and, indeed, of the need to change the economic system. I was an academic teenager and by the time I was 14 or 15 I was reading Marx and Lenin and so on. I was never allowed to join a political party because my parents disapproved and thought I was much too young to take an active part in politics and by the time I was old enough to decide for myself democracy had been overthrown in Austria by the putsch of the Dollfuss party. The Labour Party was made illegal and that was the end of it for me. Four years later Hitler invaded Austria and as a Jewish family we had to leave although we did not actually go until 1939.

I was lucky in that my immediate family were able to emigrate at the same time as I did and we all came to England together and settled in London. I've lived here ever since. I'd begun to study chemistry at the university in Vienna but I had to start all over again at Battersea Polytechnic and eventually took a degree course. We lived in Carlton Drive, Putney then but were bombed out in 1940; none of us was hurt but the house was a total write-off. My father got compensation after the war.

I'd met an engineer from Vienna, Erwin Hauser, and we were married in 1941. We had a fairly hard time during the war years but I graduated from London University in 1944 and then I worked for a firm of chemical engineers. After the war we decided to have a family and my two daughters were born in 1946 and 1947. We had returned to Putney in 1947 and we lived in the same house for the best part of 30 years. At about the same time we became naturalised British subjects and one of the first things we did was to join the Labour Party. For quite a long time we were not active members, I had a young family which kept me very fully occupied and I returned to work when my children started school. Erwin was also working very long hours.

It was not until about 1958 that we became interested in the Campaign for Nuclear Disarmament; we joined in the marches and there we met Anne Kerr who urged us to push the nuclear disarmament cause within the Labour Party. We both started going to ward meetings regularly. We soon became quite involved; I became Branch Treasurer and have held the office ever since, to this day!

We joined in the routine work of the party and on the whole we found it a satisfactory form of political activity. Of course, there have been times when I've felt frustrated but we can't all be Generals, there have to be some Indians too. I've had a busy life outside the party; quite a successful professional career and a busy family life and all sorts of other interests. I've always done my share of the donkey work of the party and I've never had any ambitions to become a Councillor or anything like that; certainly not to make a career of politics. I prefer the supporting role.

In the early sixties when you were the choice for parliamentary candidate of the nuclear disarmers in the party we ran into the unhappy business of the official enquiry which was wished upon us. I felt at the time that the so-called right wing (I don't like these labels but we all have to use them for brevity) that they acted very unwisely; it was they who caused the split by pushing the issue to such an extreme point. They did not realise that the nuclear disarmers were acting from moral conviction; they failed to understand our point of view and we failed to convince them of the earnest commitment of our position. However, the breach, bitter though it was at the time, healed eventually and when you became our candidate and Ian McGarry our Agent, the party took on a new lease of life.

The Putney Labour Party is not extreme but it has always been left of centre since then and I myself am slightly left of centre though not as much so as some other members of the party. The area of agreement in the party has always been wide enough for me to feel confident and happy as a member of the Putney GMC. Today, I find myself differing from the majority of my colleagues on the question of an incomes policy. Even when you are very far from a fully planned economy, incomes have such a crucial effect on inflation; and inflation is an evil which falls harder on the poor than on the wealthy; that the Labour movement must accept some type of incomes policy. I think the question was badly handled by our last government but I did not disagree with what they were trying to do.

I think it is justifiable and inevitable that those people who do most of the work in the party should have the greatest influence in forming policy. No one would agree to do the drudgery if they did not have the

chance of occasionally making their point of view felt. The changes
under discussion, more influence for party members, are at present the
subject of adverse comments in the press. It is said that a tiny minority
wants to run the party; but these are the people who do the work. It's
not an exclusive club and in my opinion it is quite justified in any
organisation that the voices of those who work in it shall be heard
more than those who are only passengers; indeed, it is almost inevitable.
There are many members of the Labour Party, and for ten years I was
one of them, who just pay their subs and do nothing else at all. These
people should not be despised if that is all they can manage but those
who go to meetings must have more influence in forming policy and
they are entitled to that influence.

Current trends in the party stem from the nuclear disarmament
period and although the issue itself has fallen into the background with
the spread of nuclear arms to many nations, I really believe that if
Britain had adopted the policy of unilateral nuclear disarmament this
might have given a moral impetus to the whole question. If our
example had been followed and today only the two superpowers held
nuclear arms the world would be a safer place than it is. I still think we
should stop playing with Polaris and other lethal and expensive toys of
that nature for in no circumstances can it be right to use a weapon
which cannot be aimed in space, because it affects such a large area and
which cannot be aimed in time, because the consequences go on for
generations.

Today the Labour Party is absorbed in local and national affairs and
ignores international issues to a great extent. I am as guilty in this as
anyone else but in some ways it was good for the Putney Party to be
involved in local issues when we gained control of the Wandsworth
Borough Council. Through members on the Council the party had an
influence on local affairs and that can still be seen and felt in
Wandsworth today.

I am a party member because I think there is a lot wrong with the
world and I could not live with myself if I did not feel that I was
doing something, however little, to change that. I like the
companionship of the party too. I've made a great many good friends
and, certainly since my husband died and both my daughters
married, this companionship has come to mean a lot to me. I think
we're lucky in this party in Putney in that most of the active members
are very likeable. I can't say that going round putting leaflets in
peoples' doors is particularly satisfying and trying to make members
is not an activity one enjoys for itself but these things are necessary and
doing them together makes them tolerable. Discussion can be

interesting, not necessarily always so, of course. I get impatient when things are not run efficiently but this is sometimes unavoidable especially with voluntary organisations. I am impatient with the member who does no work and compensates for this by half-baked ultra-radicalism. I dislike canvassing and am always upset when I find someone who tells me he has always been a Labour supporter and then follows this up with a barrage of reactionary opinions. Meetings are less dull than they used to be now that we limit the business and spend more time on political discussion.

I have the impression that our active membership is becoming increasingly middle-class, many are graduates on quite good incomes. We are not as successful in enrolling the young weekly wage-earner. We must look into this; it's very important. One of the things I've enjoyed about party membership is that it has given me the opportunity to go on school managing bodies which I find very interesting and very satisfying and recently I've joined the Community Health Council. Here again, I feel that a lay person, not involved in local government, can play an active part in the community and can do something to help people, which is really what it's all about.

ALF BARTON

63. Born in Putney and has lived all his life in the Thamesfield Ward.

Not only was I born in Putney myself but my wife as well and our parents and grandparents were also Putney people and perhaps even before that. I went to All Saints' School off Putney Common and attended All Saints' Church where my wife and I were married during the war.

I was a trade union man first of all and when I joined the Putney Labour Party as an individual member I was President of the Wandsworth Branch of the Amalgamated Engineering Union. I was also active in the Trades Council and the Borough Labour Party which existed at that time. The constituency parties were being established about then and a chap in my branch called Percy Stewart who came from the North of England asked me to join him in helping to build up the Putney Labour Party. At first we had no Putney HQ and we met down in Wandsworth but there was an old stalwart called Mr Reed and old George Wyver and one or two others and somehow we got the party established and eventually got our own HQ at 168 Upper Richmond Rd.

I worked in a factory in Earlsfield during the war; they were on government contracts and we forced them to adhere to the fair wage clause in the contract. That was how I became active in the AEU. They tried to sort us out and they soon found there was no work for me and I got put off. Then the factory came out on strike and I was reinstated but in the meantime I had got a job with London Transport and I've been with them ever since. I maintain the brake equipment on Underground trains.

I was one of the first Chairmen of the Thamesfield Ward and was on the General Management Committee of the party from its early days. I fought the Thamesfield Ward for the party at thirteen Borough elections and always lost; eventually I was asked to stand in Southfields and I won there in 1964 and at that Borough election we also won Thamesfield for the first time. I was on several Council committees and at the same time I was President of the Trades Council and Secretary of my own AEU Branch.

At the end of the four-year period we were all defeated in Southfields and it was fortunate for me, healthwise, that we did not get re-elected. I was definitely overdoing things at that time, for immediately prior to that I was Chairman of the Putney Labour Party during the period in which we had all the rows over your adoption as parliamentary candidate. There had been several abortive meetings but I was determined that a candidate should be adopted and I managed to push it through in the end. I was in the middle and not committed to either of the two contending groups but the wounds were soon healed and we won the 1964 general election. That was the pinnacle of my political aspirations. I grew up in Putney and I saw it change from the Ranelagh polo grounds to the Barn Elms Estate. At one time all that area was exclusive to the use of the upper set. I knew that one day it would be ours and when the constituency was won for Labour that was a great day for me. What a change! I remember my own father used to say, 'You must vote for the people with the money!' We changed him and many other old people.

In 1970 I was appointed a Justice of the Peace and I decided to concentrate on that and to keep up my interest in the hospitals. I had 21 years with the Royal Free Group and then I accepted nomination to the Kingston and Richmond Area Health Authority and I'm still a member of that body.

We've had many old stalwarts who've put a lot of work into the Putney Labour Party over the years. Old man Reed was a pillar of strength, there was the postman, Reg Chambers and his wife, there were the Munns, all the family, Mrs Lee and Mrs Haskell, Bert Rentle, Arthur Snowdon and his family and the Kennedys, people like that who you could rely on and who would work and work and work. We could not have won in 1964 but for the work put in over the years by people like these. But don't forget also the help you got through Equity from all those stage and television people; they were the stars of the day, they helped us to raise money, indeed I think we made a profit on the election. I remember Annie Ross and Edna O'Brien coming to speak for you at a school hall here in Thamesfield Ward where I was in the Chair and there was Alfie Bass and Clive Dunn and people from 'Emergency Ward 10' and 'Z-Cars'. It was marvellous.

I remembered then taking a delegation of people to the Town Hall just after the war to protest at the delay in making proper repairs to their bomb-damaged houses. We got the workmen on the job two days afterwards. That sort of thing gradually built up support for the party and that's what made the difference in the end.

VIC LOCK

Age 63. Draughtsman in electronics. Married, one daughter, married and away from home. Wife's health has deteriorated recently and Vic has to care for her much of the time.

I was first a trade unionist and joined the Communist Party. We put up one of our members as a Labour candidate for the Council and got him elected but were hauled over the coals by the CP Head Office. I remember a girl came down and said 'Nobody resigns from the CP, comrade.' So I resigned and joined the Labour Party. I've been a member of the Putney Labour Party for more than 30 years and during that time I've seen the Southfields Ward, where I live, wax and wane and then grow again many times. In those early days Mrs Jeffries and her son used to run the ward. There were seldom any meetings and we just became active at election times. We had no hope of winning Putney even in 1945. Our candidates did their best but Putney was not winnable in those days.

In the post-war period I was very active in my trade union and the Labour Party came second but in recent years I think the party has taken first place. We have more full-time officials in the union now and they do much of the work which used to fall to me as Branch Secretary but I still hold the job as well as being Chairman of the Southfields Branch of the Labour Party.

During the war I knew something was wrong which had to be put right and I came to think that the Labour Party could do it. Before the war I worked at the Cafe Royal. There was an election on at the time, I suppose it was in the thirties, and a big chap who worked there asked me how I was going to vote. I knew nothing except that the boss was a Tory MP so I said 'Conservative, I suppose.' This chap hit me and knocked me off my feet, 'Don't you ever let me hear you say that again', he said. And I never did.

My activity has mostly been in my own area. Sometimes I was almost alone in being active so I really couldn't give it up because there was no one else to do the work but there are great rewards. The night you got elected in 1964 we sang at the top of our voices all the way home after the count right along Merton Road. We had achieved something.

Another satisfaction is in looking after branch members, getting Councillors to take up their problems, arranging for a home-help and so on. On the other hand when the party gets into power it somehow doesn't come off. Hope dwindles and you begin to wonder what you've been working for. Labour Governments seem afraid of the press; we lack a paper of our own. We should take no notice of the other side, just get on and do what we want like the Tories do when they're in office. We should be more resolute. Our last Labour Council here made a mistake in timing. They increased the rates in election year. The Tories wouldn't have done that and now they're in and we're out. Our party's getting a bit too middle class.

I've had some influence on local affairs and sometimes you get a resolution through the General Management Committee. I turned down nomination for the Council many times. I just did not fancy it. Working for the Labour Party is important to me, a part of my life, I must enjoy it or I wouldn't keep on. I sometimes feel like a parson with his flock. People often ring me up and ask me to raise matters on their behalf. Of course, I've been Chairman of the branch for about ten years and we have regular meetings with varying attendances; it goes up and down. I've got a lot out of my Labour Party and trade union work. It's given me confidence. I'm basically a very shy person but nowadays I meet people and get up and speak and chair meetings without any trouble.

In the Labour Party you meet all kinds of people. You call at their houses to collect their subs and have a chat about things and over the years I've found how to do that. So I've got great satisfaction out of my Labour Party work even though I've been disappointed in some ways. Perhaps we pitched our hopes too high and expected more than was possible. The Health Service is important to me and it's good but not as good as it ought to be. The Labour Party is about people not only about policies. Being in the Labour Party got me elected on to schools management boards. I'm very fond of children and I enjoy that work. I'm now Chairman of Sheringdale and Vice-chairman of West Hill and it's very rewarding to see the children growing up and getting on.

I'm often about and children get used to calling me Vic or Uncle Vic. Now they've been told they must call me Mr Lock and one girl said to me yesterday, 'I don't know what to call you now Mr Lock-Vic.'

*51. Born in Portsmouth. Married in
1946 and then came to London.*

First we lived in two rooms in Earls Court. We were on the LCC
housing list and eventually they found us a home on the Ashburton
Estate here in Putney. We had two bedrooms and I already had
Margaret and David, and John was born there. At the time I thought
that completed my family but there was a postscript later.

A couple of years after that we were moved to the Alton Estate. At
that time Roehampton was not a ward on its own, but was part of
Putney, but the party was very active there and we became involved in
such things as delivering leaflets. I was helping a friend of mine who
became a Councillor, Leslie Buck; he got on the Council and I joined
the party. That would have been about 1961. Leslie decided to leave
for Canada and he suggested I should try to get on to the Council
myself. We were members of the same Church and he said that the
Labour Party would support someone like me. I roared with laughter
because I didn't know anything outside my own family but he
persuaded me to think about it. Mr and Mrs Buck were leaving
because he had been offered a good job as an educational psychologist in
Canada and I did think about being a Councillor but not very
seriously. Still I kept going to ward meetings and then they were
selecting for the Borough Council and people who came hoping to be
selected were talking about London things and national things; they
didn't seem to me to be talking about Roehampton things. I was
having a moan about this after the meeting and someone said it's no
use moaning about it why not put your name forward and someone
else said that I might as well because I wouldn't get chosen anyway.
So I said alright and put my name forward thinking I would have a
sort of dummy run to see how it worked and I went all through the
procedure and the end of the story was that I was one of the three
chosen to be candidates for the ward. The Putney Labour Party were
absolutely fantastic; they supported me tremendously because I
really didn't know anything about the world of politics but I did
know my own locality because my kids went to the local schools,
I shopped at the local shops and we went to the local hospital — all
those things and I found that this was what the Labour Party was
all about, listening to ordinary people like me. And I was actually

elected to the Council! That was in 1964.

When I got all the papers I was bedazzled but then I realised that there were things like Welfare which meant the old people and disabled people and the Children's Committee which I felt I could offer something to and I went on those committees and soon I was Vice-chairman of the Children's Committee! I was amazed but it seemed that the Labour Party could use the ordinary qualities and knowledge I had. Then I got a real shock — I discovered I was pregnant! So shortly after I had been elected — I was really downcast. I thought it was a shame because people would say 'Oh well, there you are, that's a woman, why elect a woman they immediately go and have babies.' But I went back to the Putney Labour Party and explained the position and they wouldn't hear of me resigning and said they would support me all the way and in fact they did and I stayed on and after six weeks I was back. Ann's early childhood was being taken round children's homes and old peoples' homes — she was a great asset to me not the other way around. So that proved to me the Labour Party didn't say 'Oh, you are a nuisance, go away', they supported me at all times all the way through. They were really good, you know and I felt really encouraged by this because I would have been distressed to have left because people might have said that in future they wouldn't choose women of child-bearing age because they might go off and cause by-elections.

We lost in 1968 but I was back on the Council myself, top of the poll in Roehampton but of course, we were in opposition. Still, most useful I found for *because* we were not involved in policy-making on a large scale I was able to do quite a lot on a personal level, taking particular cases up and all that. After that I thought I would pack it in; I'd been on seven years and I thought I ought to spend a bit more time at home so I did not stand at the next Borough elections. We got back with an enormous majority; that was in 1971 and they'd hardly finished counting the votes before they were on the 'phone saying, 'Look, we need your experience, will you please come back as an Alderman!' So I asked the family and they said, well it was your idea to give up in the first place, so I went back as an Alderman and a year later I was asked to be Mayor of the Borough! That was 1972/73 and I had a very exciting and hard-working year as Mayor. It was really enjoyable though and my parents came up from Portsmouth and were so excited that this should happen because when I said at first that I was going to stand for election they thought I should be put in the Tower because people like us didn't do things like that. So, of course, when I became the Mayor they were very, very thrilled. They were always Labour and my father trade union and they had a terrible time in the thirties.

After I was Mayor I became Chairman of Social Services and that was another very interesting but very hard year. During that year we laid down our ten-year plan and then my career on the Council came to an end because my marriage came to an end and I had to become the breadwinner and the person at home. Ever since then I've been what I started out as, Labour Party member, deliverer, ward attender and so on — just one of the rank and file.

But nearly ten years ago the Labour Party put me on the panel and I was appointed to the Bench and I'm still a Justice of the Peace.

Do you think your involvement in political work had anything to do with the break-up of your marriage?

No, I don't. No. Definitely it was not. I first became involved when my interests were purely my husband, my home and my children and he used to look further afield even in those days. I thought it might be because I was a pretty dreary sort of person but as events proved, through the Labour Party I went on to become, I think, you know, quite an interesting person, and he *still* went off with somebody else. (Laughs heartily.) So, I think my political activities, if anything, probably preserved and prolonged my marriage because it gave me an interest of my own, I became a person instead of being Bill's wife and Margaret's Mum and David's Mum and John's Mum, I was *me*.

I was always very close to my ward. At one time I was Treasurer of the Ward and for most of those years I was a member of the General Management Committee of the party. I can't remember *not* being on it. In the group on the Council there were many divisions and a lot of trouble and even on the GMC we often disagreed but in Putney I never felt that there was any bitterness. I often didn't agree with what the majority were saying but I was never made to feel that my views weren't valid. I appreciated that.

There were often tremendous rows on the Labour Council Group. I remember your Marie and I were brought before the leadership and officially reprimanded because we voted against rent increases on one occasion. There was often a good deal of bitterness in the group but I never found that in the Putney Labour Party. I was very naive at first, I actually went round on a loudspeaker saying 'Vote for a Labour Council and with the Labour Government we will keep rents steady' and, of course, practically the first thing they had to do was increase the rents. I voted against it because I felt I was committed to do so and so did many other Putney Councillors who were also carpeted. When we came to the Tory Housing Finance Act I was Mayor and because it was law I felt I had to vote for it. It was very difficult.

We've always had a lot of social occasions in the party. We were a very jolly group. We used to have things we called 'Mug and Cushion' parties. You'd take along a mug and a cushion and hold free-ranging political discussions in peoples' houses in Roehampton. They were often held at Maureen Proudman's because she had a larger house. I was very close with members of the party who also belonged to the same Church as I did; there were quite a few members of Holy Trinity in the party. At one time Frank Tompsett was Chairman of the ward and there was Leslie Buck and Betty and Norman Knights and others. They were good days.

The most important thing that happened to me was to become a Justice of the Peace because even now there are very few working-class people on the Bench; people who do a job and look after a family; they are nearly all their own bosses. The most important thing I did was to put my name forward as a candidate which showed that somebody just like me could go forward and with the help of the Labour Party, do what I have done. In the Labour Party there is a sense that with other members you can achieve things. Of course, when I was more active the more you did, the more you were expected to do. That was a problem sometimes, people would say 'subs haven't been collected', or 'ward notices have to be delivered' when you were trying to do six other things. The actual work falls on the few but I don't think that's particular to the Labour Party.

Now I'm what's called a 'Domestic Administrator' with the Inner London Education Authority working at the Polytechnic of the South Bank; what used to be called a Bursar, looking after the students and the accounts. At one time I was Governor of Elliott School, Chairman of Heathmere and of Beavers' Holt. I once became a Manager of the Roehampton Church School but I gave that up after a year because it was impossible to change anything there and I only went on it to try and change things. I was the only Labour member. When I went to work for ILEA I had to give up all my school appointments because of the rule that employees cannot be on school boards. It seems such a waste to me — such a waste — because this rule applies even to women who are serving dinners or cleaning the school. I could understand a rule which said you could not be a member of the governing body of the school in which you worked but I can't understand this blanket prohibition. It seems such a pity, people like Dora Holmes who is an aid, she helps the teachers — not allowed to sit on any of the managing bodies of ILEA. Crazy, crazy! My daughter's a youth leader and has two children at school, deeply interested in education, more than willing to give her time, yet like all of us — excluded. Doctors are not excluded from Health Authorities. It dosen't make sense and usually the Labour Party does make sense I find.

Now that my children have grown up I've been interested to see the way, I hope without any undue influence from me, except by example, they've become very involved. The older ones are all members of the Labour Party and are actively involved in community work. My son is on the steering committee of the new community centre that's supposed to open in Beaumont Road, my daughter's chairman of a local tenant's association, all very much involved in the local community. Two of my children are married, my elder son, interestingly enough was an 11-plus failure. He went to Elliott Comprehensive because it was the nearest school. I had no wild ideas about what education should be, I'd left school at 15 but he went there and the teachers took an interest in him and he passed seven O levels and three A levels and won a place at university and graduated from there and he's now a consultant geologist. When I saw what that school did for him I became very involved in the world of education and that was why I was on so many different schools and active in so many different ways because I really didn't feel I could do enough because if they could do that for my son, good oh, let's do it for a lot of other kids as well.

SID GOWLETT

*A retired statistical clerk, Sid is the longest-serving member
of the Putney Labour Party. After war service he joined in
1947 and has been continuously active ever since.*

My father was a Labour voter and a trade unionist but he never joined
the party. I've lived here most of my life and because I've remained
single I've never had the distractions which take people away from
party work. After the war I felt the pages of history were really going
to be turned rapidly. I thought we were in for a social revolution and
the workers would take control. I wanted to get in on this but could
not find the Putney Labour Party but eventually discovered a
Mr Joe Grinyer of Gatwick Road in the Southfields Ward of Putney.
He told me they met over the Co-op store in Wandsworth High
Street.

In those days everything was conducted in what struck me as a
pompous and formal manner, nearly all male, with fat trade unionists
standing up and orating with their thumbs in the armholes of the
waistcoats and watch-chains across plump bellies. Petty personal rows
were frequent but after a couple of months I was asked to become the
Ward Secretary and soon after that I was on the General Management
Committee of the whole party and on its Executive Committee as
well. I was plunged into a local election and soon found my way
round with a little help from older hands.

The work of the Putney Labour Party became my chief spare-time
occupation and it has remained so ever since. I have been Chairman and
Vice-chairman of the party and for the last fifteen years Treasurer.
My other hobby is watching cricket.

Over the years the party has changed. There are now fewer factory
workers and more white-collar workers and of course, many more
women. Nowadays people call each other by their first names; then it
was Mr or Comrade. Things got very hostile when the Campaign for
Nuclear Disarmament tried to get control of the Putney Party for its
policies and succeeded. There was a strong rival group in the
Campaign for Democratic Socialism which was outraged when the CND
people carried a resolution to take the party banner on the
Aldermaston March in 1963. I was Chairman for part of this time and
held the party together as I did not belong to either group. Neither did
Alf Barton who succeeded me as Chairman in 1963. The CDS group

complained to Transport House and there was an official enquiry. You were, of course, a leading member of the CND group and became their nominee for the parliamentary candidature. When you were elected in 1964 and Ian McGarry became Agent, the party grew up and wrangles were less bitter.

I was elected to the Council in 1964, was defeated later and was made an Alderman in 1964. When Labour controlled the Council the party became less involved in national affairs but my early hopes and expectations of great change were gradually disappointed and I immersed myself in day-to-day problems. Hopes were revived when Labour came to power in 1964 and for a time there were great expectations but they waned away again. I decided to stick it all the same – by that time it had become a way of life with me. I did not drop out nor did I move away from Putney. Some people who did may be working away in other parties.

In my early days I used to talk politics in the office and became known as a socialist. I may have done my prospects some harm. I don't know but most people were non-political. Not interested except at election times.

I don't think I've influenced the Labour Party. I went to Annual Conference one year as delegate but my impression was that it was all fixed up in advance. I went to a compositing committee and it was clear that the mass of resolutions enabled the officers to get a composite out of it, or sometimes two composites, which covered the ground but left precious little of your resolution. If you stick out your motion would probably not get reached and would fall. Of course, you could challenge it but generally you felt they'd done their best to get the sense out of the heap of resolutions on the subject. That was the year when Aneurin Bevan was off the Executive and in the body of the hall and all the cameras were on him. They took little notice of the platform. I suppose you could say that rank and file does influence the leadership very indirectly but in the end they seem to go as far and as fast as they think best which is not very far and not very fast. But over the years, of course, we've seen great changes. These have been when the party has been of one mind, leadership and rank and file working together. But we still live in a profit-seeking world.

MRS LEAH HARVEY

Lives in Roehampton with her husband. Dr Philip
Harvey, a Consultant Physician in the National
Health Service. After her children were grown
up Mrs Harvey studied law and became a barrister
at the age of 53.

I've been a socialist since my teens but I didn't join the Labour Party
until after we came to Roehampton in the fifties. A friend and
neighbour Mrs Elizabeth Mitchell suggested I join but the great
galvaniser in those days was Anne Kerr who lived in Roehampton
and represented Labour on the old London County Council. I was a
nuclear disarmer and Anne organised a group 'Mothers Against War'
to go to Geneva and I went with her. Also I marched to Aldermaston
each year.

At that time I was on the General Management Committee and we
had a great struggle with Transport House to get you adopted as our
candidate. The party was investigated and although it all came to
nothing it was terrible while it lasted. I remember we formed a
Women's Group in Roehampton and one of its objects was to
support your candidature.

I was born in the East End of London. When I was a girl at school a
group of us formed what we called the Secondary School Students
Socialist Society, if you please. We used to do our homework at
Whitechapel Reference Library and meet and talk there; it became
almost a University of Socialism. We were active in the Aid for Spain
movement and we also took part in many anti-Fascist marches
including the demonstration in 1936 at Aldgate that stopped
Mosley's blackshirts.

Lately I've not been active in the party. Since I became a
barrister I've been too busy but perhaps when I retire I may take up
more party work again. I enjoyed my period on the General
Management Committee; it was an interesting and exciting time and
we discussed a very wide range of topics. Putney made itself known
nationally and we sent strong resolutions to Annual Conference; we
also chose you to represent us in Parliament. When your voice was
heard we felt you were our voice too.

JACK HAYWARD

*Born in Bow. Came to Putney after the
war. Age 69. Now retired.*

The Putney Labour Party was very small when I joined after the war.
We had our meetings in pubs or school halls. That was in 1946 and
soon after that we began to collect money to get our own
headquarters. I was already a member of the party and had been for
many years before the war but George Wyver was the driving force in
the Putney Party in those days. With the help of Mrs Chaplin or
Miss Marcuse as she was then who was a parliamentary candidate for
Putney in those years eventually enough money was collected to put
down a deposit. We scrubbed the place out and repainted it and
brought it into use. That was 168 Upper Richmond Road.

For most of the years and up to today I have represented the
Electrical Trades Union on the General Management Committee of
the Putney Party. I've seen the party grow in those years, success and
failure. Our victory in 1964 was made possible by the growth in
council housing in the constituency. Sometimes we collected money
and at others we were penniless. Putney used to be very reactionary
but the more left wing we grew the more successful we were
politically – the more victories we won. I'm left wing myself – as
Aneurin Bevan said, we must get control of the commanding heights
of the economy.

I'm still a member of the Clarion Cycling Club and secretary of the
South London section. Robert Blatchford was our founder and his
'Merrie England' was very influential years ago. I worked as an
electrician for the government, Ministry of Works, Property Services
Agency they call it now. I've got a medal for 25 years service.

I don't think much of George Brown. In the East End we marched
against Fascism in Spain in 1936 and against Mosley. We put gas
masks on to show people what war was like. The Fascists threw a
child through a plate-glass window. Clem Attlee was the member for
Limehouse in those days. That Mosley tried to intimidate the Jews but
we stopped him in Cable Street. I was on the Wandsworth Trades
Council for about ten years. Years before then when I was young,
George Lansbury used to take us down to Hyde Park in a dust cart
– that was for May Day. The Co-op gave the kids buns and milk.

I met my wife in the Clarion Cycling Club after the war. We lived

here in Putney but she was a Salvationist and she didn't like my love-
making so it didn't last and she left me and afterwards we were
divorced.

KEN TIPPING

*Telephone engineer. Was married and had
two children, now grown up and away. Now
divorced.*

When I was first married we had nowhere to live but were on the old
LCC housing list and in 1954 we were offered and accepted housing on
the Ackroyden Estate here in Putney. I came from a Labour family and
joined the party when I lived in North Kensington and I re-joined soon
after we came here. I was not immediately active except at election
times but when the family grew up a bit I found time to go to ward
meetings and became a collector.

I quite enjoy going to ward, or branch as we now say, meetings; it
keeps you in touch. I only got on to the General Management
Committee quite recently and was quite impressed with the level of
debate. As a collector of subscriptions I wish we had something, a
booklet or journal would do, to hand over in return for the sub. I
sometimes feel embarrassed at being empty-handed; we don't take the
trouble to keep our members fully informed.

There's one thing that worries me and it is that nowadays Labour
always seems to be on the defensive. In 1945 we had a programme and
people could follow it, it was positive but since then we've been pushed
into the position of always seeming to be defending ourselves against
attacks constantly made on us whether we are in power or not. It
seems to be that we got our information over better in those days than
we do today when the Tories always reap the benefit of work done by
Labour Governments. I think a bad press over the years has done us
harm.

I can't say that I like canvassing. I think the doorstep is the worst
possible place to try to convert anyone to anything. As for the local
paper the *Wandsworth Borough News* is so hostile that no one likes to
see their name in it; it's like being in bad company.

I hold firm political convictions and my membership of the
Labour Party is a part of this; I think I am more interested in local
than in national politics but I have never wanted to be a Councillor
myself; that's not my cup of tea. As for conflicts within the party, it's
only natural that there should be differences of view which have to be
thrashed out. There's one thing that worries me and that is that I
think we're losing too many members and failing to make enough new

members. People come to Putney and Roehampton from all over London and leave their roots behind and if we don't get hold of them they grow away from us with improved living conditions. The activities of cowboy trade unionists last winter lost us a great deal of support; I know because people told me so in very strong terms. For myself I think loyalty to the party is very important and without it nothing can be done.

LEN HOLMES

*Age 61. Quiet and reserved but with the self-possession
which comes from long experience of people and
their problems. Is occasionally moved to write
very good letters to the local paper.*

I was Chairman of the Putney Labour Party for three years from 1969
to 1971 and before that Vice-chairman for two years. I work for the
Post Office but as Branch Secretary spend most of my time, by
agreement, on trade union work. I have been around the Labour
movement most of my life but I did not actually join the Putney
Labour Party until 1959. Before that my wife and I used to work for
the party at election times without actually being members.

I was born in Wandsworth and my father, Johnnie Holmes, was a
well-known leader of the unemployed workers' movement between the
wars. He was a great character but no one would employ him and so
with seven children and my mother dying of cancer we had hard
times. My wife was born not far away in Wimbledon.

I left school at 14 but did some more study at night school after
that. In 1938 I joined the Territorial Army when Chamberlain came
back waving his magic piece of paper. I went through the Dunkirk
episode and after that I did four years in Burma and the day we
returned to England they were announcing the results of the 1945
general election. When he found Labour was winning, the captain of
the troop-ship turned off the Tannoy system so we could not hear the
details. That was my first vote – Labour, of course.

I was thoroughly disillusioned with Winston Churchill and the
wartime government. We had seen the conditions people had to live
in in India and we knew it was time for a change. We thought we were
voting for a new system. That's how many soldiers saw it.

I worked as a labourer for a time with the Wandsworth Council
when I was demobbed and after that for London Transport on the
Underground. In 1949 I joined the Post Office and I've been with
them ever since. The Post Office, by agreement with the union, allow
time off for public service work and this allowed me to stand for the
Council in later years.

Dora and I married soon after the war. We did a short period in
private service so that we could be together and then lived for a while
with her parents. Our first home was a Nissen hut off the East Hill,

found for us by the Wandsworth Council after pressure from Jimmy James, a Labour Councillor who had known my father. Then we were moved to Armoury Way and finally to our present Council flat in Castlecombe Drive in 1962. We had four young children at that time and Dora did a lot of election work while she was very pregnant.

I first stood for the Council in 1968 but was not elected until 1971. I was made an Alderman in 1974, one of the last non-elected Council members, and stood again in 1978 when we were defeated. In 1974 I was also Deputy Mayor.

I enjoy representing people, looking after their interests. I do this in my trade union work and I did it on the Council. Also I'm Chairman of the Governors of three schools and have been for a dozen years now. I've been on the Executive of the party for a similar time and Chairman of the West Hill Branch since 1963.

I think the link between the Labour Party and the trade union is essential. I don't think Conservatives can be real trade unionists.

I enjoy being in the Labour Party, being a part of it though I'm not sure that Labour has always truly represented the aims and interests of the working class. I don't go along with the ideas of the middle-class intelligentsia. This doesn't apply so much to the Putney Labour Party which has often supported the trade union movement when most of the parliamentary party have seemed not to. The government and Cabinet have certainly gone astray from us in recent years in following policies which trade unionists could not support. Still, better the devil you know. There's a lot of good sense in the grass roots of the Labour Party and the leadership would do better to take more notice of us instead of trying to tell us all the time what they think. We must hang on to the constitution of the Labour Party and particularly to Clause Four calling for more public ownership. On the other hand, I don't think the rank and file should spend time attacking our own government when we have one; that helps to let the Tories in. It's a pity we have to have a left wing and a right wing. There's faults on both sides. We need a modern form of socialism to replace the ideas of 70 years ago. It's easy to condemn our own government but the only way to change the system in this country is by having a succession of Labour Governments, one after the other because when Labour is in power everything else works against it.

You mentioned your father?

Yes, Johnny Holmes was well known as a pacifist in Wandsworth between the wars. During the First World War he drank a lot of water before medical examinations and was always rejected because this increased the pulse rate. He was a street-corner orator and he fought a parliamentary election in Wandsworth as an independent although he eventually joined the Labour Party. He was a friend of Saklatvala who held Battersea briefly for the Communist Party and at one time was a member of the Socialist Party of Great Britain. He was put in Wandsworth Prison for six weeks after leading a demonstration against Wandsworth workhouse. He marched into the institution and demanded that the inmates be fed proper food instead of pigswill. Once he lead a 50,000 strong demonstration of the unemployed to the Cenotaph. He was stopped by the police because he had a banner which read: *For those who are dead and not forgotten and for those who are here and are forgotten.* My father brushed the police aside saying that they would fight their way there if necessary and he successfully led the demonstration to Whitehall. However the demonstration was broken up there by mounted police and my father was kicked in the head. He was injured quite badly but eventually recovered and was soon attacking the Royal Family from a soapbox on the corner of Magdalen Road. My father wanted clean sheets and bed linen for the workhouse inmates and porridge and bacon and eggs for breakfast. When he was taken to Wandsworth Prison there were demonstrations outside every night with singing of the Red Flag until the authorities removed him to Brixton. When he came out there were several thousand unemployed to meet him and they marched all the way to our house in Wandsworth.

Quite apart from the fact that there was no money for it, my father did not believe in paying rent to private landlords and was always being taken to court for non-payment. He accumulated £500 in arrears and never paid it. He argued his own case and the landlord said he wished my father was on his side. He was a very clever man. He studied what the magistrate had said on other occasions and quoted him. Once he was offered a job on condition that he changed his politics but he would have nothing to do with capitalism. He was an ardent socialist and knew all the leaders of those days, Lansbury, Greenwood and Bevin but he became a bit disillusioned with the Labour Party. They were not nearly socialist enough for him.

For myself I think there is no real alternative to the Labour Party; whether you like it or not politics will affect your life and only by taking part in political activity can you try to influence the course of events in the interests of the people you are seeking to help.

MRS VERA THOMPSON

*Widow. Age 51. Husband died two
years ago. Had two children but
both died young. Now alone but a
strong and cheerful personality.*

It was my husband who made me a socialist. I was an orphan, brought
up in a convent. Then they put me out to foster. They put me with the
Vice-chairman of the local Conservative Party in Edgware and she
joined me in what they called the Young Britons. It was a sort of
junior Conservative League and I took part in a speaker's competition
in Caxton Hall and the local Councillor gave me five bob which was a
fortune then to me. Then I went back into the convent because my
foster-mother was cruel to me and later the convent put me into
domestic service. They were not supposed to do this I thought,
because I believed my own parents must have left some money as I
was one of only four in the convent who were taught shorthand-
typing and book-keeping. I was supposed to get further education
until 18 but they chucked us out earlier because it was during the war
and they were taking in a great many refugee children from abroad.
The good old LCC got me out of service and put me in an office job
in town and then I met my husband and we were talking politics one
day and I said that if I voted I supposed I'd vote Conservative and he
said 'Don't you let any of my friends hear you say that.' And he
really told me off. He was great on the trade unions. He never
actually joined the Labour Party himself but he was shop steward on
the Ashburton Estate when that was being built. He went up there
right from the start; he wanted the experience of seeing the finished
product right from digging the drains. He was a steward with the old
plumbing trades union. He lectured me every night about socialism
until he got me to change my mind. (Laughs.) After that I became a
better socialist than he was! He had TB and at the time we were in a
damp basement in Chelsea. He had a lung collapsed, we were on the
LCC list and a doctor at the Brompton Hospital told the Medical
Officer of Health that my husband could not be sent back into the
conditions that caused the TB. Within a week we had the offer of
a maisonette in Roehampton. At that time I had Billy who was about
three and Lester my eldest who was away most of the time because he
was a mongol. We made friends in Roehampton and one of them asked
me if I was a member of the Labour Party. I said no but I vote Labour

and she said you must join and she got me the form and I filled it in and joined and she used to drag me down to the meetings. I remember going to the branch to choose Jean Standing as one of our Councillors. My friend was a German girl who had married an English soldier — she was very strong on the Labour Party. I didn't really understand what was going on at the meetings, about Standing Orders and things like that. A little political education for new members would have been a good idea. Anyway, eventually I was asked to be Secretary and I did that for three years and I've been on the General Management Committee of the party for several years now.

I used to be on the Wandsworth Tenants' Joint Action Committee and I was one of the wicked ones who burst into the Town Hall at the time of the Tory Housing Rents Act. I think Putney Labour Party is a bit middle class. In Roehampton Ward we tend to be working-class people and sometimes we feel a bit out of place when we go to the GMC because we are not as articulate or as well-educated as many of those on the GMC from other wards.

Some years ago Marie suggested that I should go on the Council panel. She said, 'It's people like you that we want.' And Jean Standing said, 'I left school at 14.' I always believed that if you're a Labour Party member you should be active and although I thought I was not knowledgeable enough I thought over what Marie said and when my son Billy got killed on the A3 and Lester died — but being a Mongol that was on the cards — I decided that instead of sitting at home feeling sorry for myself I would go on the Panel and then I was chosen for West Hill and then for Southfields. We lost both those elections but then I was chosen for Roehampton and, of course, we won there in 1978 although we lost the Council. It is extremely frustrating although it must be worse for those with experience of having been in power before.

I remember working for Dick Taverne in 1959 and now I'm glad he didn't win for it would have been terrible if he'd done in Putney what he did in Lincoln. It was a great day when you won in 1964. I remember going canvassing with someone from 'Z-Cars.'

I like Labour policies. We stand for equal opportunity for everyone. I work at the Surrey County Council in Kingston in the Architect's Department on a computer terminal, I do programming of design work and costing out. I'm not only on the GMC of Putney Party, I'm also on the Executive Committee. On the Council I'm on the Social Services, Recreation and Public Accountability Committees. I never have any time to myself but really I like it that way. I like to advance the cause of Labour and

I'd like other people to feel the way I do about it. To me it's almost unbelievable that anyone should live on a Council estate and vote Tory.

I'm very active in my trade union, the National Association of Local Government Officers at work and because of this I have never been able to make much progress. If ever I go for a higher graded job they always say to me, how are you going to carry out the duties of this post when you're always away on NALGO duties? I'm the Welfare and Social Secretary and on the Executive and a delegate to the South-Eastern District Council and from there to the National Committee on Equal Opportunities at NALGO HQ. I'm delegate from the branch to Kingston Trades Council and from there to the London Association of Trades Councils. I recently went with a delegation from there to Moscow. I'm also a member of the Co-operative Party and I'm delegate to one or two other organisations.

I think the Labour Party ought to involve itself more closely with the local community, like the Liberals used to try to do. Perhaps we've got a little bit too complacent.

The old LCC was a very good landlord but there's no regular inspection with the Tories, you only get something done when things go wrong and then you have to wait. I shop locally and people know me. I expect that's why I finished top of the poll at the local elections.

You've come a long way.

Yes, when I was at school they noticed that I didn't want to do PT. They found out I was covered with weals from my neck to my ankles. My foster-mother had beaten me with a dog-whip. They didn't take me away then but it happened again. One day another girl and I went knocking on doors looking for our real mothers. The police picked us up and we were both beaten and I was told that my mother was dead anyway and that was the first time I knew my mother was dead. Then I got another beating for asking my foster-mother what would happen to me if anything happened to her. So eventually the LCC took me away and I went into another convent. So you can see I had a real right-wing bringing up. When I was being fostered, the LCC provided very good clothing. My foster-mother chose a very pale green velvet dress for Kathleen who she also fostered and a cherry red velvet dress for me. When they came she told us to put them on. She said Kathleen looked lovely and then she said 'Look at that! Whatever could you put on *that* to make it look anything? You can take that dress off, that will do for

Kathleen next year.'

It was a terrible shock for me when my first child turned out to be a mongol.

SAM DOUGHERTY

Rubicund and jolly-looking; for years Sam
played the role of Santa Claus at Labour Party
Christmas Bazaars.

1962 was a key year in the history of the Putney Labour Party; we
adopted you as our parliamentary candidate, we gained control of the
Borough Council and we got a first-class Agent in Ian McGarry. The
party came to life and began to play an influential role in the Borough.
Before that, out of 60 Councillors we had only 3 so we had no
influence or voice and played no significant part in local affairs. All of
a sudden in 1962 twelve Putney Councillors came on to the Wandsworth
Council and by that time Anne Kerr was our representative on the
London County Council. Overnight we were in a position to help
people and Putney began to take off. Then, in 1964 you won the
parliamentary seat and Putney was ready to play a prominent part in
politics at all levels. We had a Labour MP; a Labour LCC Member and
nearly a quarter of the Council. Today we have turned full circle; we
have none of these things; we are back to our three Councillors.

In 1965 the new London Borough of Wandsworth was formed and
we held our twelve Councillors; we played a great part in forming the
new Borough. The Labour administration which controlled the
Borough from 1965 to 1968 did great work, a tremendous slum
clearance effort and a great re-housing drive, we made mistakes but the
Borough was transformed.

We lost in 1968, largely because of the Wilson Government, but
returned in 1971 to carry on the good work. Labour Councillors in
those years included many capable people; there were the
Brownjohns, Alan and his wife, the Tilleys, John and Tracey, Ian
McGarry, Brian Sedgemoor, Christopher Helm, Martin Linton, David
Grugeon, Max Madden; it was a Council of all the talents, there was a
tremendous spirit, morale was especially high in 1971 when we
returned after our earlier defeat. Perhaps there's a good omen there.
In 1971 Ian McGarry became Leader, I was Group Secretary, the
Deputy Leader and Chairman of the Housing Committee, David
Nicholas, all of us Putney representatives, this Council again did great
work and more should be known about it.

Where were you born?

I was born in Liverpool: my father was a merchant seaman and he was a great friend of the Braddocks, he emigrated from Liverpool to London, I say this because we were treated like immigrants. He came after work like they do and the London kids called me a dirty foreigner because of my scouse accent. We had fights and I got a black eye so I have always felt for immigrants ever since then.

At 14 my mother died and I ran away to sea. I worked in London before that riding a bike for the Home and Colonial Stores; twelve shillings a week, from eight in the morning until seven at night and nine on Saturdays. One Friday night I came home, gave my sisters the money, except for three shillings, stole my elder brother's overcoat and hitch-hiked to Liverpool and got a job going to sea as a deck boy. My pay was £1 a month and my first trip was to Australia. While we were on the way there the war broke out.

I was torpedoed three times. The first time was a ship called the *Scottish Maiden* in November 1941. We were right in the middle of the convoy. We had a mixed cargo, benzine in the first two tanks and crude oil in the other four. I came off watch at four in the morning. I always used to go down into the galley and get a cup of coffee but this morning, for some reason I went straight up to the fo'castle head where we slept. It was a lovely morning and at twenty past four the torpedo struck right into the galley area where I would normally have been having my coffee. We had ten minutes to get off the ship. Sometimes you wonder why it is things happen like they do.

I came out of the merchant service in 1946 and my wife and I went to live with my in-laws in Putney, Felsham Road. We had married in 1942 and had two babies. I was on the Wandsworth housing list and I went along to see the Tory Mayor, Bill Willison. He asked me if we were prepared to leave Putney and I agreed, if that was the only way to get re-housed. A few weeks later I got the offer of a two-bedroomed flat in Dulwich from the London County Council. I asked the Labour controlled LCC, the finest housing authority there has ever been in the world, if there was a chance of moving back to Putney. Two and a half years later I got a letter from them in Dulwich asking if I would like to be housed on their new Ackroyden Estate then building in Putney and in 1953 we moved into a maisonette there. We were the second family to move in. There I joined the Labour Party and, of course, I've done almost everything since then, including being Mayor of the Borough.

Joining the Labour Party was natural to me because I'd delivered leaflets in Liverpool when I was seven years old. The first thing we did

on the Ackroyden Estate was to set up a tenants' association. The first
tower block was opened by Reggie Stamp in 1954. Anne Kerr was on the
LCC by then and she was closely involved. The tenants' association ran
garden fetes and Anne took part and we got a hall on the estate and in
1956 I was asked to fight the election for the Wandsworth Borough
Council. We lost then but soon after other estates were built. We lost
again in 1959 but won in 1962 and then came the years of Labour
control. At the 1962 municipal election the three West Hill candidates,
Mrs Brownjohn, David Grugeon and myself, all did a tape recording
and we broadcast that from a loudspeaker on a car parked nearby,
while we were knocking on doors canvassing, so people could listen
to us talking about what we hoped to do and then question us on it.
We also spent a bit of money on a better quality election address.

The party went through a rough time after that with deep
divisions on the nuclear disarmament issue. Looking back it was rather
silly — all that enquiry business at Transport House. I kept out of it.
Most of the CNDers were good party people and I didn't think it
was worth while splitting the party in the effort to oppose them. But
tempers ran high at the time and at one ward meeting one member hit
another over the head with an umbrella! The GMC was divided into
two separate groups but curiously enough some good came out of it;
it livened the party up and showed that there were things we believed
passionately about. When we won control of the Council in 1962 I
remember Marie saying to me, 'Now we can let them have a
Council room to hold CND meetings in.' Soon after that we abolished
Civil Defence.

The first Labour Leader of the new Council was Sid Wellbeloved
and the Deputy Leader and Chairman of Housing was Sid Sporle. I
was Vice-chairman of Housing. When Bob Mellish was appointed
Housing Minister he came down and asked us to double our housing
target. The only way we could do this was to go in for
industrialised housing and tower blocks. Rippon kept up the pressure
in 1970 and it really was the only way to build quickly. Tower
blocks have become greater problems than need be because of the
decline in the quality of housing management consequent on economy
drives. At that time the Borough was in a desperate plight from the
point of view of housing, there was no room to build anything in
Battersea and so we simply had to build up in Putney and
Roehampton; slum clearance demanded it. For a long time we got no
subsidy from the government for rehabilitation, only for
re-building and so we had to pull down places we would have
preferred to do up. Eventually we got subsidy for conversion but

before that a lot of quite good homes were pulled down.

We were a pioneer housing authority and so we made some mistakes but I'm still not ashamed of some of our estates in Putney and hundreds of people are still glad to be there out of the slums. I lived on one myself and I know. I only moved out because I was living in a five-bedroomed place when the family had grown up and we needed something much smaller, so the Council got the benefit of those extra rooms.

The balloon went up in 1968 and Sid Sporle went to jail. I believe that he was simply trying to be a full-time Housing Chairman without the means to do it and that if allowances to chairmen had been paid then at present day rates Sid would never have been tempted to take doubtful money — the forerunner of the Poulson affair. From most points of view Sid Sporle was a first-class Housing Chairman and although we lost in 1968 in 1971 we were back in full strength with a Council which consisted for the most part of entirely new people. There were 45 of us and only 10 with previous experience; most of the new Councillors were young and eager and many of them turned out first-class. In addition to those I've mentioned there were Dave Nicholas who was to become Chairman of Housing and whose report on housing 'Arithmetic of Despair' made such an impact. Then there was Len Holmes, Jean Nicholas, Mike Williams who succeeded Dave on Housing, Peter Ackhurst, Maria Marshall, Dorothy Smith, Hugh Stephenson who was Business Editor of *The Times* and experienced Councillors like Bill Carney and George Rowe and Amy Bush; there was Tony Belton who eventually became Leader of the Group and many others. In our first 100 days in 1971 we stopped the sale of all council houses, extended concessionary fares to all pensioners, we helped to kill the motorway through Wandsworth, we sold the Mayor's Rolls-Royce, we developed the direct Labour force, abolished all library charges, established consultation with the tenants' associations with working panels in each of the areas, we brought the free milk for children back in spite of Mrs Thatcher, we increased the grant to the Community Relations Council; we developed social services and within a fairly short time we established Wandsworth as a place where those who needed the care of the community were looked after; that was socialism.

Then in 1972 the Tories clobbered us with the Housing Finance Act designed to force us to increase rents; we were divided on whether we should defy them or not; the leadership which wanted to stand up to them was defeated with the aid of the Tories.

Franks Sims became Leader for a very short time and many of us resigned our positions including Ian McGarry and myself but before long we were back again and we carried on the good work and in 1974 we were returned with a larger majority.

Perhaps we should then have consolidated but we went ahead, up went the rates and we did not get our case over, we should have concentrated more on maintaining our stock of housing and built a little less; we should have put our direct labour force on maintenance instead of putting it out to private contractors. The old LCC used to get such work done by its own people on the spot but contractors kept people waiting, estates began to run down while we were concentrating on building new blocks and our own people began to get fed up. We were also blamed for squatters and for families with problems. Nobody had a solution; the Tories pretended they had but we were in charge and we had to carry the can. People found out that squatters were jumping the queue for housing and we got the blame for that too. Together, these things brought about our defeat in 1978.

I was Deputy Mayor in 1972/3 and Mayor in 1976/7 and I've experienced most of the joys and sorrows of Council work so I think it right now that I should stand aside and let the youngsters take over. For years people have been knocking on our door all the hours God sends and I think my wife is entitled to a rest. I believe that people should be active in the party and in the Council at the same time and that, generally, is how our people have played it in Putney. Even then, the link between the party and the Council was not as close as I should have liked it to be.

When the new London Borough, including both Wandsworth and Battersea was first formed, the Battersea end resented Putney's loquacious young Councillors but later on the new Council jelled together and that feeling died down but certainly, for a time, Putney Councillors were thought of by old Battersea hands as a politically motivated elite. We were led by a first-class debater in Ian McGarry and Putney Councillors tended to dominate Council debates.

Although I've now retired from the Council and from the General Management Committee of the party I'm still active in other ways. I'm Chairman of the Governors of a large Comprehensive School at Southfields, I'm a member of the Area Health Authority, I'm on the management boards of three other schools and I'm a governor of a large technical college, so I'm still quite busy.

What about your private life?

When I left the merchant service I joined London Transport as a bus conductor; in 1954 I joined the GPO as an ordinary postman. I took an examination to become a counter-clerk; in 1965 Tony Benn decided to set up the new National Giro bank and I was appointed one of 30 officers to get it off the ground. The opposition was very fierce but we succeeded in the end and in 1972 I took up my present post as a telecommunications consultant with the Post Office.

As for the party I sincerely hope that once again we shall avoid a serious split. We can do so if we start attacking the Tories instead of each other. Labour should now be defending the Post Office against the Tory plan to split it up.

All the well-known London Labour figures have been in my house canvassing over the years, Herbie Morrison, Bob Mellish, you name them.

Let's get back to your personal life.

Well, we had three daughters and a son. They all went to the local comprehensive school, one got a degree in law, one went into accountancy, one went into art as a designer and my son is an executive engineer with the Post Office. Mary and I now have six grandchildren.

I was eleven years old before I had a pair of shoes of my own. We shared second-hand shoes, used them for Sunday School or the Band of Hope and on Monday morning they were pawned; my two brothers and I used to take turns to go to the pawnshop, Uncle Kehoe, we called him, because it made you late for school and you got the cane. It was quite normal to be barefooted and I have better feet now for it. My wife always compliments me on them. At school I could not afford the halfpenny for a cup of Horlicks and those of us who had no money were sent out into the playground while the others had their hot drink indoors. That's what made me a socialist. Never did I think in my wildest dreams that I should end up as Mayor of one of London's largest Boroughs. People today do not know what poverty is. My mother used to go pawning for other people who were too proud to be seen there. They would pawn their suits or sheets off the bed or blankets or their pensions books, one man used to pawn his docker's hook for threepence to buy a packet of Woodbines and a penny cup of tea. This was poverty in the twenties and thirties. What strides have been made by successive Labour Governments. People just don't believe it today.

LADY ELIZABETH MITCHELL

Widow of Sir George Mitchell. Has lived in Roehampton for more than thirty years.

We came to Roehampton early in 1948 so I saw the whole of the Estate being built. At that time Roehampton was a small village; there was just the common and what is now Danebury Avenue was parkland and a farm owned by the Jesuits at Manresa College. It was like living in the country, there were farm noises and priests directing pigs along with sticks; it was an unusual suburb with very few shops, most of them very expensive as they had a virtual monopoly. When I joined the Labour Party, which was just after I got through my Bar examinations, we were a part of the Putney Ward. It was dispiriting, the ward was so right-wing you couldn't get a progressive resolution through, you hadn't a hope in hell – it was really a most depressing business.

When the London County Council built the Alton Estate Roehampton became a ward on its own and a working-class one but in those earlier days there was no one on the left at all. Later on when Anne Kerr, Clark as she then was, came to live in Roehampton in Medfield Street, she and Maureen Proudman livened things up no end, that would be in the later fifties; I joined the Party in 1953 and they came a year or two later. We lived in the same road in Roehampton as the Conservative MP Sir Hugh Linstead, and every time he won he used to put up a huge notice saying 'Thank-you Putney' which was extremely irritating. One election the Conservatives put an election address through my door and to make the children laugh I tore it up and stamped on it but when Hugh Linstead returned home with his loudspeaker, the children went out and told him what I had done which was a bit embarrassing!

I thought Linstead was a good MP but having you for the last 15 years has been highly satisfying. There was not a single political issue on which I felt I should write to you (except commercial radio) I think you and Marie were a first-class team.

The Campaign for Nuclear Disarmament brought the party together a lot in the early sixties. I was a founder member of the Putney and Roehampton CND. By this time we had our own ward in Roehampton and it was much more progressive than Putney Ward

67

which made me feel more at home. Now, of course, the area has been divided again and I'm in the unwinnable West Putney Ward.

I have been a socialist ever since Penguin Books published Bernard Shaw's *Intelligent Woman's Guide to Socialism* which converted me overnight. That was back in the thirties and I used to take the book to school in my satchel. I first joined the party when I was at Oxford – the University Labour Club. I have a grown-up daughter and son – both socialists – and am a grandmother.

The Putney Labour Party underwent a marvellous change in the early sixties; Anne Kerr became our LCC member and eventually we got you as our parliamentary candidate – not without some trouble. At that time I was a member of the General Management Committee of the party. We formed a Women's Section in Roehampton with the main purpose of getting a few more votes to cast for you at the Selection Conference, although, in principle, I don't agree with Women's Sections at all. It folded up not long after. I remember there was a complaint about this and an investigation from Smith Square. I remember the investigators coming down and a GMC meeting being attended by what looked like a couple of heavies. I remember the day of your selection very well with that nerve-wracking system of the exhaustive ballot in which candidates are eliminated one at a time; we won through, thank goodness.

Some years later, I think it was in 1968, I resigned from the party because I disapproved of Callaghan's Immigration Bill and the way he put it through in five days without proper debate. I remember I wrote to you telling you of my decision to resign and you replied saying, 'Too bad but you'll go on giving legal advice at my "surgery" won't you?' I thought what a bloody cheek but, of course, I did carry on though I found it a bit annoying when I had to answer 'Putney Labour Party' on the telephone when I wasn't even a member! Once someone rang up and said, 'Tell old fuzzface' – that was you – 'to drop dead!'

I certainly felt the free legal advice we gave was worth while. At that time it was difficult to get local solicitors to act for people with the sort of problems we got. Some of these were eventually dealt with by the local law centres. We had a hell of a lot of cases, didn't we! I think matters improved with the local solicitors later on and the cases tailed off so that I could deal with them by domiciliary visits which was more satisfactory in some ways – for example, you could get away from the client!

I re-joined the party after a year. What alternative is there? There's nowhere else to go. It's not very satisfactory but if you're a socialist what else can you do? One thing about the Labour Party, it's a wide spectrum and there's room for one.

Some people think the local party has swung too far left. I've not been affected by it but the decision to push Pamela Aylett off the governing board of a comprehensive school because one of her children had gone to a fee-paying school (for special reasons) was very much resented by some people; not only because it was done but because of the way it was done – she turned up at a meeting and was told to go home because she wasn't a governor any more.

I find it difficult to make up my mind about this business of making the party more democratic. I think it's right that more people should have a hand in writing the manifesto and in electing the Leader but if you look at the way people on the National Executive Committee are themselves elected, there's not much democracy in that. Union members of the NEC are elected by mass trade union votes. At the time I was in the Transport and General Workers' Union (I worked in aircraft production during the war) there wasn't much democracy there with mass votes being cast for me by Ernie Bevin.

My husband was extremely active in the Popular Front in Scotland before the war, organising meetings, speaking on the Mound but he withdrew from politics altogether after Munich and, as you know, he became a senior civil servant. When Chamberlain sold out Czechoslovakia George resigned from the Labour Party and the Church of Scotland. When he joined the Border Regiment in 1939 I think he rather hoped he wouldn't survive the war.

What else have you done?

For over five years from 1958 I was London Area Organiser of the Family Planning Association, after that I became a law lecturer at a Polytechnic; from 1968 until last year I was active in running the Pregnancy Advisory Service, one of the two charitable abortion organisations which provide cheap abortions for people who, for various reasons, can't get them on the National Health Service, and so fill a gap. I did a lot of broadcasting between 1962 and 1974 giving legal advice on the BBC 'Can I Help You' programme. I was also on 'You and Yours' and on 'Woman's Hour'. Now I'm a part-time Chairman of Industrial Tribunals but with the present government's policy towards employment protection I don't know how long the job will last. I've never seen a government quite like this in the whole of my life – I'm 58. I don't remember any other so right-wing and so dogmatic. It seems that they intend to wipe out everything good that has happended since 1945. I've been a Justice of the Peace since 1966 having been put up by the Putney Labour Party. The training is not bad but I don't think justices are told enough about penology. I'm saying that because I took a four-year course in criminology and have a great interest in the question of penalties and their effectiveness. The majority of justices do, when the crunch comes, seem automatically to prefer police evidence if there is a conflict of evidence. I suppose I may be doing some good by staying on the Bench but after 13 years I find it a bit of a losing battle. I was a member of the Roehampton Community Health Council when it started but I resigned because I couldn't spend enough time on it. I'm glad that Marie's been appointed.

In my job as part-time Chairman of Industrial Tribunals I sit as a legal Chairman with a member representing the TUC and a member representing the CBI. We deal with such matters as complaints of unfair dismissal, redundancy claims and so on. If the present government's proposals go through there will be quite an erosion of employment protection rights. It's all rather sad. I feel rather like Mervyn Jones in that article in The *Guardian* – one remains a socialist but without hope.

HARRY BLANKS

Age 63. Londoner. Born in Willesden.
Re-housed in Roehampton after the war.
Labour Party member all his life.

I married after the war and we had three children. I had to go into hospital for an operation and after that the medical people came round home and saw I was living in a basement in Paddington and told me we should be moving out within a fortnight. And so we came to Roehampton. I have always been in engineering and got a job locally with KLG, now Smiths Industries and I've been there ever since. We've got a new name now, it's Smiths Aviation Defence Special Unit; it's an aviation division of the Smiths Group. I've always been in this area and am doing much the same job now as when I started with them 22 years ago; now I'm making parts for the framework of the Concorde engine. We still make special plugs for aero engines.

I joined the West Willesden Labour League of Youth when I was a boy of 15. We came to Roehampton in 1957. Anne Kerr was very active in those days and she knocked on our door before our packing cases were undone. She had been told that I was an active member and she said, 'Let's see what you can do for us'.

For several years I divided my time between Roehampton and Paddington where I was still busy. I've raised hundreds of pounds for the Labour Party in my time, perhaps thousands, all kinds of activities from collecting subs to running dances, selling Christmas cards and so on. I stood for the Council a couple of times in Paddington but not in seats which were won at that time. In Putney I soon became a delegate to the General Management Committee from the ward but nowadays I represent my union, the AUEWE, on the GMC.

Although Roehampton is the safest Labour ward in Putney nowadays, our organisation today is not as good as it was, there are not as many active workers. I do more trade union work myself because I'm now Branch Secretary. I've been a shop steward as well for much of the time but recently they decided they wanted someone more militant. The new man still has to come to me for advice.

I stood for the Council in Putney Ward and we had a good fight but, of course, lost in that unwinnable ward but when I was put forward for Roehampton I was turned down by my own people. I thought I would get at least half of the 32 present but all I got was 8 votes. I told them that if that was all they thought I was worth they could go out and do the work I had been doing and I withdrew from activity for a year. I came back because I saw that all I had built up was falling apart. I've built it up again but it's not as good as it was.

I'm a socialist at heart, I love meeting people, I love discussions about problems and I love trying to solve difficulties and improve things. I've taken up the Chairmanship of the branch but it seems harder to get people to work these days; it's like hitting your head against a brick wall. Still, we have regular branch meetings and usually get a dozen or so there.

I don't believe you'll ever nationalise the banks as long as there's a white man standing on British soil. I'm not a militant. The Swiss banks would stop all that so you'd have to have international nationalisation.

Although Roehampton is the strongest ward in Putney politically it's very weak in members today and if the subscription is raised to £5 a year we shall lose most of them. Contributions should be increased a little every year and not a lot at once. The people don't like splits in the party; when I go out collecting I talk to the people as well and get to know what they are thinking. People believe what they read in the papers so it's a pity we lost the *Daily Herald* and *Reynolds' News*. People say 'Don't bother to call no more' but I turn up next time and sometimes they've forgotten it. But not the race thing. That upsets them and I had one man join the National Front.

We have no trouble of that sort at the factory. We have all sorts there but we're all one really but put an umarried black mother in a flat, she gets visited by a man who stays with her and she's on social security and then you've got trouble, especially when our own people are still waiting to be re-housed and the children cannot get anywhere to live when they grow up and marry.

I tell people to buy the *Labour Weekly* but they don't although it's not a bad paper. What's happened to the Co-op, they seem out of politics altogether these days. They used to issue a free newspaper.

The Conservatives will save us. In spite of everything, you see; there's going to be a lot of trouble and within a year or two we'll have a Labour Government back.

What did you do in the war?

I was in the Desert Rats which later became the Eighth Army, first in Egypt and after that in Italy. We were under Auchinleck and Ritchie, the two worst generals we ever had. I had a lot of arguments in the Army because of my political convictions. I was taking six-pounder field guns to Turkey to repel a mythical Russian invasion while we had only two-pounders camouflaged to look like six-pounders to fight the Germans with.

*33. Married to Ian McGarry (q.v.) One young
son. Formerly Chairman of the Putney
Party.*

I come from a Labour family and can remember being involved in
elections around the age of nine. It was a natural thing. My mother has
been active all her life and is a Labour Councillor now; my sister works
for a Labour MP in the House of Commons, is married to the
Secretary of the Co-operative Party and was also a Councillor.

I joined the Young Socialists when I was 16 and became Secretary
and later Chairman. There were only a few of us but we played an
active part in the party as a whole which, unfortunately, the Young
Socialists don't seem to do these days. In the early sixties we were
active in supporting your candidature for the parliamentary seat and we
got blamed for the resolution which was carried by the GMC deciding
to take the party banner on the Aldermaston CND March, although it
actually came from the Thamesfield Ward and was supported by us.
In a way, we were happy for this to be so. This was followed by the
National Executive's decision to conduct an enquiry into the affairs
of the Putney Party as the result of which the officers of the Young
Socialists, including myself, were forbidden to hold office for a year.
In fact, the YS reappointed the same officers at our reconstituted
meeting after the enquiry and nothing happened. We had been
summoned to Transport House and all our minutes and membership
records were examined. We were producing a magazine at the time
Young Left which we sold on the Aldermaston March. This was held
up and waved at us by our examiners who included Ray Gunter and
Arthur Skeffington. It all seemed innocent and matter-of-fact to us
but we were asked what did we mean by this and what did we mean by
that. It was a sort of 'When did you last see your father?' situation. I
remember two articles you had written for our magazine were
mentioned.

All this was brought about by an anti-CND group in the party who
protested when we selected you as our candidate and complained to
Transport House. The NEC was recommended by its Organisation
Sub-committee to defer endorsement of your candidature but they
decided to endorse you and to have the Putney Party investigated. In
those days we had a physical division in the GMC with the CND people

sitting on one side and the anti-CND group sitting on the other side. It was pretty nasty at the time. After the enquiry we got away with some sort of censure and no one was expelled. All this was followed by our victory in the 1964 general election and that saw the unifying of the Putney Party. To have a Labour MP pulled people together and all the preceding uproar was more or less forgotten.

When the 1964 general election campaign started the party agreed to pay Ian McGarry the salary he was getting at his bookshop job to act as election Agent for a period of three or four weeks but when we won he stayed for 12 years! Ian and I were married in February 1964; there was a Borough Council Election in the May, and Ian was among the Councillors elected, and the general election in the October, so it was a pretty busy year for us. I had worked since leaving school for Transport House and then in the Labour Party Regional Office. Later I worked for the Wandsworth Borough Council and after leaving to have my son, I became a Councillor myself. That was for Tooting, in 1974. I found it pretty wearing with my other commitments and although I enjoyed the work, four years was enough especially as Andrew needed a good deal of my time about them. Throughout the years I have been on the General Management Committee and a good deal of the time, Branch Secretary as well. I couldn't *not* be involved in Labour Party work. I've been Chairman of the party for the last two years and I shall be giving that up soon but I hope to remain on the GMC.

During the years I've often been disappointed in the performance of Labour Governments; for example, their attitude to pay policy, immigration and so on sometimes tempted me to tear up my party card but I've always decided it's best to stay and try to change things from within.

Have you enjoyed being Chairman of the party?

Yes, very much. I found it a bit daunting at first. I was aware that there were some people waiting for me to make mistakes and I made some and had to backtrack pretty quickly but the experience has given me much more confidence. I've had quite a bit of experience in the Labour Party. I went to Annual Conference regularly as part of my job. Last year I went as delegate for the party and found that fascinating.

Looking back I think one of the greatest issues locally was over the Housing Finance Act. Most Putney Councillors were against implementation and this caused difficulties between us and the rest of the Borough. After Ian resigned as Leader the Borough seemed to get into a shambles. He and the others who resigned with him were asked to return. He agreed to do so although I was against it at the time but now I think it was a wise decision because we could not hold out forever and at some stage we were going to have to implement the Tory Act anyway.

I think the present Labour setback both in the country and in Putney is only temporary. The way this government is acting people are going to be pleading for us to return. People who voted for them at the last election never expected anything like this. I think we shall regain Putney too and control of the Council. Putney has often been one step ahead of the rest of the country and perhaps we shall be again. Your successor is turning out to be a dead loss — people here aren't used to having a part-time MP. We may recover control of the GLC before then.

I hope the next Labour Government will have learned from the mistakes of the last one. They will have to carry out their election undertakings to the full and must never let down the people who put them there again. In Putney we had what I thought was a rather worrying period when branches seemed to stop bringing resolutions to the GMC and we had little political discussion but now the resolutions are coming up from the branches again which I'm very relieved to see. I think we're fighting back and getting on our feet again politically in readiness for the next fight.

IAN McGARRY

Assistant General Secretary of Actors' Equity. Was Secretary Agent of the Putney Labour Party and Leader of the Wandsworth Borough Council.

When my family moved from Lewes in Sussex to Putney in 1961 I was already a member of the Labour Party and active in the Young Socialists and in the Campaign for Nuclear Disarmament. When I got on to the General Management Committee in 1962 you and Marie were established members and so were Russ and Anne Kerr. I joined the Labour Party because I wanted to be active in it. I was keen on the CND but wanted to be involved in wider political issues which could only be dealt with by the Labour Party. Trade union activity also seemed to me to be a part of the wider struggle. The trade unions in the last few years have been at the centre of politics. On the whole they have been more effective than the Labour Party and I think I see my future in that direction though I know some people thought of me as a future Member for Putney.

I became your election-Agent in 1964 because the Party wanted someone to work full-time just for the period of the election campaign. I gave up my job in a booksellers a few weeks before the general election on a promise that the party would employ me until such time as I found another job. And then we won, of course. Transport House decided we were worth a bit of money and the party wanted to keep a full-time Agent and so I stayed there for thirteen years! And got married.

Of course, a year earlier, in 1963, there was all the uproar about taking the party banner on the Aldermaston March. I think the momentum generated by that extraordinary business might have helped us to win in the end. The Organisation Sub-committee of the National Executive wanted to censure the officers of the Putney Labour Party and I was one of three members recommended for expulsion. This was never acted upon nor were any reasons given but this all made the active members of the party that much more determined to win the election. We had been put on, not a McCarthy type trial, but the nearest the Labour Party could get to it. We were all challenged to prove our loyalty to the party, which we never thought was in question, and required to justify our support for CND. Endorsement of your candidature was also in doubt for a time.

The local party thought, very well, we'll show you — and we did. In the end we got the candidate we wanted and a lot of people were very steamed up.

You can't compare that 1964 result with any other. It was absolutely marvellous. There were many organisational deficiencies but these were more than made up for by the enthusiasm we were able to engender not only in Putney but among actors and quite widely in surrounding constituencies. We never had so many people and their keenness rubbed off on the electorate.

We held the seat, which had never been Labour before, not even in 1945, for another four general elections and, of course, it's nearly always more difficult to hold marginal seats when Labour is in office. 1966 was better organised than 1964 but not so enthusiastic. It was extraordinary to hold Putney when Labour lost in 1970 and the first 1974 election was a little like 1964. By then we had lost a Labour ward and so there was another win against the tide.

We lost in 1979 for many reasons but one of them was that the nature of the constituency moved slightly against us for the first time. Increased property prices meant that Labour people moved out and those moving in were not so likely to be our supporters. But the collapse of the Liberal vote was what really did for us.

Whatever happens I shall always remain a member of the Labour Party. All of us active members who care about the party have become increasingly frustrated that we never seem to achieve a Labour Government which meets the aspirations of the people who put it there. But despite all that it is the only political party worth supporting in this country and to do anything other than to vote for the party, to be a member of it and to work for it would be to betray everything I believe in.

All the same I really don't think that the nature of the Labour Party, or the future of politics in this country, is going to be determined by issues like the re-selection of MPs. These issues are quite important but much more important than constitutional changes is for the Labour Party to re-establish itself as the party of the ordinary working people of this country, the party they recognise as being their party. You can't get back to that simply by constitutional changes, it's a political problem to re-create an identity with the issues which concern the average man and woman. The most depressing thing about the last election was not that we lost but that we got the smallest vote we've had for 40 years.

Lots of people we still asume are our natural supporters did not vote for us. We have to recover them. Mrs Thatcher will help; of course.

Her government will do more to educate people about the need for socialism than any Labour Government has done since the war. But that is not enough. We have to break out of the depressing pattern of Labour Governments like the last three and this is where constitutional changes come in. When the party is in government the party outside Parliament must have greater influence in combatting the massive pressures which the establishment, the civil service and so on bring to bear on a Labour Government.

It's nonsense to pretend that there's a Labour Party which is very important when you're in opposition, which puts up the candidates, writes manifestos, gets people elected and then disappears into limbo when the party takes office and leaves everything to the party in Parliament. If the last Labour Government had listened to the party and to the trade unions we could have avoided the mistakes which led to the Tory victory.

I dislike the drudgery of the party membership; the jumble sales and boring committees but I actually enjoy routine organisational jobs like delivery and canvassing and I really take a delight in election campaigns. But the Labour Party seems to want to bore everyone to death at its meetings and why members put up with it I simply don't know. Our party here in Putney rarely gets divided on fundamental issues so there's not the disagreement which livens things up. Debates were much livelier when I joined Putney 18 years ago. Then we gained control of the Borough and local matters absorbed more of our time and leading members of the party became Borough Councillors. There were important local issues such as housing and social services and the local papers concentrated on them. I think we became over-absorbed in local issues and are only now returning to national matters since we lost control of the Council but, apart from the Common Market, the party as a whole has not been as concerned about international affairs until quite recently. While we had a Labour Government most discussions were about implementing our own policies or failure to do so. I found in local government that one of our problems was the resistance of officials to an authority which wanted to come in and change things.

Being Leader of the Council was a fascinating experience and I gave it up for purely personal reasons. I was on the Council from 1964 and was Leader for seven years. There was a brief gap in which I and others resigned over the implementation of the Tory Housing Finance Act. This issue certainly divided the party locally and nationally. I'd been 13 years party Agent. Labour has always paid badly and by 1977 I was broke. I had a wife and a young child and I decided I needed a change. There are very few other jobs which would permit me to remain leader of the Council so when I applied for the job at Equity and got it I realised I should have to give up being so active on the Council and eventually I had to give it up altogether; the pressures of the Equity job were too great.

I don't think I've had any influence at all on the Labour Party nationally, as an individual member, as a party Agent or Leader of a Borough Council. There were occasions when Leaders of local councils would meet with government to try to bring pressure to bear but not with great effect. The most frustrating thing is to see people like Phyl and Peter Courtney who are in the Labour Party, not because they want to get anything out of it, but because they want to commit themselves to it, to work all of their spare time, but whose views and opinions really carry no weight whatsoever. There's no real machinery, no way in which the feelings of those people who really do sustain the party can be taken into account at national level. You have to go to a branch meeting, then it has to go to the General Management Committee, if approved it then has to go to Conference; if it gets through Conference it then goes to the National Executive who tell the Labour Government if we're in power who then take no notice whatsoever. The bloke who, a year earlier, has initiated a resolution in someone's front room feels a bit cheesed off. He doesn't think much of this internal democracy of ours. I don't know of any easy answer but it *is* frustrating that so many people who do sustain the Labour Party have so little say. The party has a form of elitism which means that a small number of people really call all the shots and don't take enough account of the folk who make it possible for them to enjoy that power. Whether the present concentration on organisational matters will do something to put this right, I don't know. But there must also be a change of attitude in the leadership of the party because without all these people there won't be a Labour Party. I know that people in office are subject to other pressures and they have to take account of them but too little account has been taken of the views of local party activists. Some members of the parliamentary Labour Party don't have the same sort of commitment to the party as such which our rank and file in Putney feel; many of them have never done the drudgery.

Neither Tony Benn nor Jim Callaghan represents the kind of leadership of the Labour Party I'd want to see. I agree with a great deal of what Tony Benn says and I think his role in the Labour Party is an important one. He provokes debate on many of the central issues but these issues ought not to be personalised. We need a collective leadership determined to reward generations of working people in this country with the kind of government they have been seeking all these years. That will only come about with the full support of the trade union movement and the actual figurehead then would be less important. On the other hand, of course, the great quality of Nye Bevan was that he combined great intellectual powers with an unshakeable basic commitment to the Labour movement. Perhaps Neil Kinnock has something of the same quality. I have a great deal of respect for Michael Foot. He has been rightly criticised on some issues but I have always felt that, whether one agreed with him or not, he personally was utterly convinced about his own position and has always been completely honest with himself and with other people about that position.

I have found great satisfactions in working with other people in the Labour Party to try and change things for the better. I know of few things more enjoyable than that. You make real, close, long-standing friends. You can use the old corny word and say they're comrades in the same cause and you grow to like and respect them. You get a lot out of getting together and working together for something you all believe in. Also, I think both Members of Parliament and Councillors get a lot out of helping individual cases where success is enormously rewarding; to get a family re-housed, to see the homeless properly treated, to get social services expanded to help the people in real need, all that gives astonishing satisfaction. To try to put principles into practice gives great pleasure and it helps to make up in some degree for the frustration in being unable to see the wider aspirations of the party being fulfilled.

My parents moved to Wandsworth when I was three months old and I've lived here ever since. First we lived in a pre-fab just off Garratt Lane; eventually there were three children and we only had two bedrooms so we were overcrowded and I had to sleep in my parents' bedroom until I was ten or eleven years old; and then the roof started leaking so at last we were re-housed on the Alton Estate in Roehampton. As you know I now represent Roehampton on the Council and became Chairman of the Housing Committee so perhaps my long experience of living on a Council estate was useful. I lived there with my parents until I went to university and so I knew about the difficulties and frustrations which the tenants experienced and, of course, about the great difficulty of obtaining a Council house at all, although, incidentally ours was a maisonette and not a house. That personal experience plus an interest in the mechanics of housing finance and the way in which it is organised; the lack of a national housing policy; the squandering of public money in wasteful ways on such things as defence; these were some of the things that brought me into politics and into housing politics in particular.

I believe my parents were floating voters at least at some time during their lives. I remember once my father saying 'I'm going to vote differently this time, I'm voting Labour.'

I studied mathematics at Exeter University and although I enjoy maths I now wish I had studied economics or politics. When I came out of university I wasn't too clear about what I wanted to do. I thought I might enjoy teaching and was eventually accepted at Merton where I am still employed, now as Head of what we call a First School in Merton which takes children from their first schooling to the age of nine. My school is in a social priority area which has a lot of problems and, in many cases, the children suffer handicaps in their home lives.

I was always interested in current affairs. Even when I was at school I always took the Labour side in our debates and it seemed a natural thing to join the Labour Party when I went to university. I helped here in Putney on vacation in your first election campaign in 1964 and I continued to be active after that but I found the terminology rather offputting at first. Such terms as 'ward parties' the 'GMC' and so on were rather alien to me but I soon got over that and started attending the meetings and I've been active ever since. I'm settled in the area and I love Wandsworth; it may seem a funny thing to say but I do and I'm very concerned about the local environment; also I love the countryside and I love hill-walking and on holiday I enjoy nothing more than going on to Dartmoor and losing myself for a few days but when I come down to it I think of all the people who are living in conditions that are far from favourable and all their adverse circumstances and it's that that makes me sure I want to be part of this local community and it's becoming part of that community and getting to know people in the Labour Party and becoming friendly with them not only on a political basis but in personal terms as well I think that keeps you active because you're concerned about the area and working with people you like to be with. Secondly, if you ask me why I'm an active Labour Party member, I don't find it possible to be a passive member. I feel very strongly about political issues and if you feel strongly you want to do something about it and if you want to do something about it you've got to be active. (Laughs.)

I fought a parliamentary election in Hove. I knew Tony Banks who was already a parliamentary candidate and he knew that they were looking for a candidate down there and he gave me an address to write to. So I wrote off and I was invited down and had a narrow victory at the Selection Conference. That was an interesting experience for although Hove is wealthy in parts there are a large number of people there living in very bad conditions. Of course, Hove is a safe Tory seat and as that was the 1970 general election the Tory increased his majority although we increased the Labour vote. John White's offered me a free pair of shoes if I would wear them for canvassing and agree to put my name to them at the end but I turned them down! It was certainly remarkable that we held Putney in that election.

The following year, 1971, I stood for the Borough Council in Roehampton and I've been one of their three ever since. Once on the Council I followed my interest of housing and became Vice-chairman of the Housing Committee. Before that I had contributed to a Shelter publication called *Face the Facts* and I'd worked with Colin Crouch on housing research. In the next year, 1972, we had a terrible upheaval in the Council over the Tory Housing Finance Act. This basically said to local authorities 'You will put up your Council housing rents, regardless of the needs of your Council and regardless of the financial ability of your tenants to pay the increase. You will do it and we are telling you that that is what you are going to do.' That seemed to many of us a gross interference in local authority affairs and we determined to resist it even if it meant that we would be suspended. This was a very difficult decision because it meant that

Councillors would be surcharged as actually happened in Clay Cross. To the great shame of the Labour movement these Councillors have not been given the support and encouragement they should have received and to this day some of them are still paying off the surcharge and are debarred from local government office. What happened in Wandsworth was that the leadership of the Labour Group was split but eventually came down for non-implementation by a small majority. Eventually, because of the pressures, one or two people changed their minds and the decision was reversed. I then resigned as Vice-chairman of Housing, so did the Chairman, Tony Belton and the Leader of the Council, Ian McGarry. There was a lot of bitterness which was sad but understandable because passions were high, the issue was important and it was a tumultous time. The people who took over did not last and eventually Ian McGarry became leader of the Group again. In 1974 we were re-elected with a larger majority and put the issue behind us; I then became Chairman of the Housing Committee.

My wife Jean (we were married in 1969 and she lived in Brixton, also in Council housing property) got on the Council herself in 1971 and remained through the troubles until 1974 when she decided not to stand again in order to take a teacher-training course. I'm one of those very fortunate people with a marvellous wife which gives us a stable background. We live in Putney, of course, and are both politically active and before we had our baby it was said that the only time we saw each other was at Council meetings. Evidently that was not true. (Laughs.)

Quite apart from Council work we are both active in the movement. Among other things Jean is Secretary of the Wandsworth Co-operative Party which Marie chairs and we both do the usual party work — delivering leaflets, knocking-up and canvassing at election times, trying to make new members, raising funds at jumble sales and so on — that's how the party works for we have very limited means and we depend on the generosity of our own supporters. I don't enjoy jumble sales but that's how we make a little money. At various times I've held ward and party offices but had to give that up when I became Housing Chairman in 1974.

Now we're in opposition and it's a pretty grim experience. You can win every argument, you can be sure of your facts, you may trip up the majority party and their policies and show that what they intend to do will be harmful to the local community but when the vote comes you lose. But we shall be back.

Perhaps you will turn your attention towards Parliament?

Possibly. I don't know. It's very difficult to forecast the future. But whatever happens I hope to remain active in the Putney Labour Party. There are occasions when it's been pouring with rain and I'm cold and wet delivering leaflets when I think harsh thoughts about the party but usually I am very conscious of the fact that the Putney Labour Party consists of a bunch of tremendous people who give their own spare time quite selflessly for their ideals and people who do that are to be looked up to. I think the Putney Party is unique. I am sure that other people think that their party is unique in some ways but in Putney for many years there has been a close identity of opinion between our MP and the party in the constituency. Party members watch their MP very closely and other Members have forfeited respect by talking one way in the constituency and voting another way in the House of Commons. Here there has been identity of view and action on such matters as opposition to increased defence expenditure, against nuclear weapons and opposition to cuts in expenditure on such things as education, health and housing. Secondly, the Putney Party has built up a close relationship with our supporters in the constituency. We've had a good organisation under Ian McGarry (and this constituency could not have been won for Labour without it) and we've maintained that relationship with Labour voters in spite of the unpopularity of Labour Governments — the general election of 1970 was an example.

Now we've lost an election and we've got to make sure that our relationship with our supporters holds good. This has been helped by the fact that the Putney Party has always had a sense of mission, of campaigning, of looking forward to the future. We've had open-air meetings off Danebury Avenue, for example and we've always tried to involve people in what we are doing and the Putney Party has always been a living organisation; a party not afraid to debate political issues and one which always rallied round at election times and gathered together large numbers of people who put in a lot of work. We're better than other parties and I hope we always keep ahead.

DR PAMELA AYLETT

*Consultant psychiatrist at
Westminster Hospital and at Queen
Mary's Hospital, Roehampton. Married
with four children. Husband, a top
executive with International Computers
Ltd, is also Labour.*

We came to Putney about sixteen years ago but after that we went North for a couple of years and I was on the Council at Knutsford. This was a Council with a so-called Independent majority but they behaved like Conservatives. When the Liberals supported Labour we could sometimes win a vote and this occurred on such things as cultural matters on which they were sometimes better than some Labour members. Now that we have reached a higher material level the Labour Party should start worrying a little more about such things.

I came from a Labour family. My grandfather was a stonemason who had seven children and earned about 30 shillings a week; he had to walk five miles to work and then do a twelve hour day. His boss would pass him on the way in a pony and trap without giving him a lift. He finished up with bronchitis and a double hernia from working on roofs. Grandfather was a Liberal and there was some friction between him and my father who became Labour. My father would have liked to be on a farm, he left school at the age of 13 and after a few years as an agricultural labourer he went to work on the railways, first as a cleaner and later as a fireman and engine-driver. He became Labour when he went into the town and in his young days was much more left than he is now; once he even refused to stand up for the National Anthem! He was anti-militarist at the time of the First World War and very enthusiastic about the Russian Revolution.

I gradually became politically aware; my father was on strike in the General Strike and there was much friction in the family at the time. Soon after he endured a wage cut and I shouldn't be surprised if we soon come round to that again. Because I was an only child we managed a cheap if limited diet and seldom went hungry; not enough milk, not enough fruit but father grew all his own vegetables. It never occurred to me to be anything other than Labour.

My maternal grandfather was very much opposed and nobody discussed politics when he was around because it stirred up a lot of pain and animosity.

I was very enthusiastic when the Attlee Government got in after World War II, at that time I was a medical student with little time for political activity and I was not really active until we went to Knutsford some years after I was married, although I had become a member of the party long before that. We had young children and were both at work with heavy jobs so there was little time for political activity. In Knutsford we lived in a street with beautiful Italianate houses and it was thought rather odd that people living there should want to join the Labour Party. When we did, they were very pleased and not only because we had a large downstairs room which was used for meetings of the party and the Young Socialists. I was asked to stand for the Council in an unwinnable ward which I did and the following year won in a better seat. It was a rather feudal town and I think I won partly because I received female support for they'd never had a woman Councillor other than one who wore pretty hats and opened fetes. I think being a doctor may have helped for it was not very political support. I was on the Health and Housing Committees and once we stopped the majority party from evicting a family with three or four children for non-payment of rent. There was a terrific row about this for it was at Christmas time but we won. I said that the family should have a visit from the Family Planning Association. This got in to the *Daily Mirror* as 'Pill on the Rates'.

Since we've been back in Putney the work load has been too heavy for us to play a very active part in local politics although I attend ward meetings when I can and last year was on the General Management Committee. I wish the party discussed foreign affairs more; these days we seem to have withdrawn into what happens in this country. I think the GMC could get through its work faster than it does; if they kept the non-smoking rule throughout the meeting instead of relaxing it at 9 p.m., they probably would! The GMC also has a tendency to cover ground already traversed by its Executive and reports could be shortened.

As compared with Knutsford the Putney Party seems to me to be a bit conformist; it is run by a group of people who tend to be bureaucratic and who support each other. I tend to be individualistic and I am not sure that this is always welcome I did not find the GMC as interesting as I had hoped it would be.

Nevertheless, being a member of the Labour Party seems to me to be the only possible approach to politics; I could never be a Tory for I was brought up in an atmosphere of Christian socialism and my father was very active in his trade union. Of course there are nice people who are Tories but I never want to be friendly with politically active Tories and I could never have married one.

I'd quite like to return to Council work when I retire if I'm not considered too old then. I came into conflict with the Putney Party once when our second daughter went to Putney High School on what was an 11+ place given by the Inner London Education Authority. Some people in the party campaigned for me to be removed from the Board of Governors of Mayfield Comprehensive and they did in fact get me off it. They were wrong because it was in fact a local authority place but the incident soured my relationship with the Putney Party.

I think all of us have some influence on the course of events, perhaps more than we know but in the Labour Party you can't influence national policy except through your local party and I don't think I've influenced the local party much; for example, on the EEC I am in a minority, disagreeing with both you and the local party who are strongly against it. I believe in strengthening international socialism and although I know there are arguments against the EEC I agree with the view taken by many socialists in Italy and Belgium, for example, who are in favour of it and I'd like to get together more strongly with them. We are getting too insular; that's my view.

The party is not attracting teenagers enough although my son and daughter were both Young Socialists and have remained members of the party. They were both too active at the cost of their studies; I think my daughter would have got a First in Economics if she had not been going to meetings too many nights a week. Our older children are idealistic Marxists and they fear the inevitability of atomic war while capitalism remains. I think capitalism will eventually go but I don't see how they're going to hurry the enormous changes needed in the complicated society in which we live; that's the problem of the next 100 years.

My elder daughter is married and has a little boy and she and her husband are both members of the Labour Party in Sheffield where they live and are quite active. The younger two children are not active but they hold broadly socialist views. I think they see the difficulties and indeed it may take many years but I think, in time, capitalism will go the way of feudalism.

RUTH AYLETT

*Daughter of Pamela (q.v.) and Peter
Aylett. Now 28 and married with one son. Lives
in Sheffield. Works with computers. Speaks with
a Northern accent.*

I was born in Ealing and when I was about nine we moved to
Roehampton. After that we moved to Knutsford for a while and it was
there that I joined the Labour Party although I was really under age at
the time. We had a big house there and the Young Socialists used to
meet in the basement. Later we returned to Roehampton and I joined
the Putney YS. I grew up as a Labour supporter; when I was very
young I remember my mother telling me the Tories would take away
the free orange juice and I was very fond of that.

In those days there was very little contact between YS branches and
we tended to be rather inward-looking. I went to meetings regularly
and remember the first issue of the YS newspaper *Left* coming out. At
that time it was under the control of Transport House and was a most
appalling paper – their idea of what constituted a youth socialist paper
wasn't all that appealing. I remember one of our members being sent as
delegate to the YS national conference and coming back quite confused
and confusing the rest of us. Being so much on our own we hadn't
much appreciation of what was going on nationally.

However, relationships between the Young Socialists and the Putney
Labour Party were good and we were actively involved in the work of
the party but we did not do much campaigning of our own among
young people. In the different areas I've lived in since it's been my
experience that most YS branches work well with their parent parties.
That's always good – the youth is the future of the party and the future
of socialism – and I've seen them working well in Colchester, Brixton
and so on. Since those days the YS has grown a great deal and improved
tremendously – they are now a functioning national organisation.
Having formulated my own political ideas I'm very pleased to see the
YS developing a cohesiveness and an impact nationally on lines I
support.

We base our ideas on Clause Four of the Labour Party constitution –
the public ownership of the main means of production, distribution
and exchange – and I remember that being described as 'Communism'
by a member of the GMC of the Putney Labour Party! I was very

impressed by the attitude of a trades unionist who said 'If Clause Four is Communism, then I'm a Communist and proud of it'! I've since come to the conclusion that Clause Four ought to be our main guide to action; it is at the root of my beliefs and should be a programme for implementation and not a piece of wishful thinking as some of the leadership appear to consider it — if they consider it at all.

The reason the campaign for democracy in the Labour Party has grown is the experience of Labour Governments, particularly, the last one. I was not so optimistic about this government as many other people were but large numbers of the rank and file had high hopes and the bitter disappointment of that government made people ask, 'What's the party for?' 'How can the leadership be so removed from the aspirations of the rank and file?' And come to the conclusion that there must be something radically wrong with the structure of the party. To believe in socialism and fight for a government to bring it about and when you get that government to find them implementing Tory policies! I know they were not in a majority but that's happened to previous Labour Governments; if you're in a minority it's better to stand on your principles and go down on those principles and then have a springboard to get in with a majority than to discredit Labour by compromising everything we are supposed to stand for. By trying to be all things to all men you become nothing to nobody. The real Tories do it better, your own supporters put you there to do something different and so you end up with no support at all.

The papers say that we rank and file activists are not representative of the party as a whole but how much support in the Labour Party do those right-wing journalists have? I've done as much knocking on doors and collecting subscriptions as anyone and I don't find this. Anyone can claim to speak on behalf of a silent majority but if you have a discussion with people and break through the headlines they read you often find that they really agree with you. You go round in elections and people say 'They're all the same. Labour politicians, Tory politicians, what have they done for the likes of us? But talk to them and you'll find that people like that are very responsive to socialist ideas. Active trades unionists who don't have time also to be active in the party, they support socialist ideas too. They are particularly hostile to wage restraint and to the attack on their living standards carried out by the last Labour Government, and the message of 'Jam tomorrow' the government proclaimed. Some older members of the party are influenced by the press and by the reds under the bed stuff they come out with but many others are glad to know that there are young people still fighting for the principles they stood for in the thirties. The press over-estimates the amount of support they can whip up with all their resources but the tragedy is that the leadership of the party also over-estimates the effect of the press and its influence while under-estimating the resources they have at their own disposal. If they were to go out and argue the case for socialism instead of acting ashamed and worrying about 'the middle ground' all the time they would soon find they could win massive support. How can they say there's no support when they never argue the case!

I think it's true that Labour has lost support both in membership and in election terms but I place the responsibility for that on the leadership of the party. If we had the kind of campaigning leadership that the rank and file deserve; if they put the energy into the struggle for socialism that some of the activists do; if they came forward and stated that they were socialists and believed in the transformation of society, not in a hundred years' time but as a practical solution to immediate problems, then they would get the response. I'm not an unqualified supporter of Tony Benn but it was very significant that when he was prepared to stick his neck out in the early days of the last Labour Government and the fury of the press was unleashed on him he got enormous support in the movement and among the electorate. In spite of the efforts of the press to lose him his seat he increased his majority quite significantly in the second general election of 1974. Where people are prepared to stand on a principled programme they have won support, for Labour people have seen something worth fighting for at last.

When I was younger I decided to take a break in further education and see something of the real world. I went to work in an engineering factory in Leeds and that was highly educational; it taught me some lessons I shall never forget. There were people probably representing the majority of people in this country condemned for the whole of their lives to do jobs they hated — boring, monotonous, deadening, soul-destroying jobs which slowly *did* destroy them. People stuck it out as best they could, like the woman next to me who used to imagine herself watching birds upon the moors while she worked, but the older people in that factory were bowed down by years of it, years of turning out 1,500 piston rings a day, it's bound to destroy you in the end. The lesson that hammered home to me was first, how much people have to put up with in this society, the — I don' know — *unbearable* way society is organised if this is the best it can provide for people; and second that while nothing can be done about it individually, collectively it can be changed.

While I was there, that factory, which was very badly organised and had not been unionised very long, had its first industrial dispute in 40 years and workers suddenly realised that they could do something about it; they suddenly discovered their own power, it was a most amazing transformation in about six months. These were not highly educated workers with a long tradition behind them at all; the jobs were low-paid, backward employment with a high turnover and a large proportion of women, but this is the reason for my basic optimism; there is no strata of workers so hopeless that they are not prepared to struggle — I shall never forget it. I believe that in the end workers have no choice but to struggle, they are forced into it and if workers like those I was with can struggle as they did then the chances of changing society are very good. If only the leadership of the party would have the same faith and optimism and willingness to struggle as the working class!

At one time or another both myself and my husband have been asked to stand for the Council or why we don't try and get into Parliament. I'm not against it in principle but my position is this. I have very definite political views, I'm a Marxist, a supporter of the paper *Militant*. I have a clear political programme, a programme I'd like the Labour Party as a whole to adopt and fight for. I don't want to put myself in a position of responsibility unless I'm certain that people understand what I stand for and are willing to support me when I stick my neck out. I don't see the use of putting myself in a leading position without that support because you get all the responsibility without the power to actually do anything. For instance, when the Housing Finance Act battle was on under the last Tory Government we advocated that Councils should refuse to implement the Act. We understood the serious repercussions which might befall people and did befall people in Clay Cross; the threat of even going to prison; we understood that people might not be prepared to put themselves at this risk since they had not been elected with this in mind. But we argued that if that was the case then they should have withdrawn and allowed themsleves to be replaced by people who were prepared to run the risks. Had it come to it I would have had no choice but to run those risks myself and under those circumstances I would have been willing to stand for the Council. Of course, it didn't come to that as it happened.

Inevitably, my husband and I can't both do as much political work as we did before we had Ben and I've had to cut down my activities. I do more work in my trade union now than I do within the Labour Party. I'm a member of ASTMS and I'm on the Trades Council in Sheffield. Obviously you can't do everything when you've got a child but there's still a lot to be done.

It is necessary to translate Clause Four of the Labour Party's constitution into a political programme for the nationalisation of the commanding heights of the economy and for some form of workers' control and management — socialist nationalisation as distinct from that applied to British Steel and British Rail. That means the nationalisation of the major monopolies, those large companies whose production accounts for 70 to 80 per cent of the national output; nowadays that means probably fewer than 200 companies. We argue that these companies, because they have such a large amount of economic power can in reality dictate to the government. We saw this with the last Labour Government. Metal Box and various other companies when Labour came in were very quick to announce that their investment plans awaited a change in policy from the government which would give them the necessary confidence; there were demands for cuts in public spending and so on. A Labour Government that really wants to implement a socialist policy will have to tackle that economic power. The nationalisation of these companies is a necessity in order to carry out the reforms that we want to see, otherwise, they dictate to us, instead of us having control of the resources. That to me explains the disastrous course of the last Labour Government from the reforms of the 1974 Manifesto to wage restraint and public spending cuts. It is said that this is too drastic a programme and that it would be better to act in a more piecemeal fashion; for example it was suggested that the top 50 companies or top 25 companeis should be nationalised for a start. I supported that as an enormous step forward in that it was proposed to nationalise profitable companies at all, but I believe if you were to do that you would face repercussions from all the other companies and, boy, they can act together when they want to, when they really feel threatened. You would annoy them without taking away their power to retaliate, and although we live in a peaceful and democratic country it would not be safe to assume that those conditions would endure indefinitely under such circumstances.

The financial and industrial sectors are interlocked very heavily now, boards of directors, the big insurance companies and so on but I still hold the view that although that is so the real power in society still lies in the control of production where the real wealth is created. The finance sector cannot stand alone and independent from production; one reason why the economy is in such a shambles is that you can't rest a strong financial sector on a weak economic production base which is what the capitalists in this country are trying to do now;

they're daydreaming. As the industrial sector of the economy declines, and it is declining quite fast, the financial sector will also tend to decline and begin to lose its important worldwide role.

The next general election will depend on what happens in the next two years and how far the lessons the rank and file have learned from the disaster we've suffered are put into effect. If we succeed in bringing about changes in party organisation so that it becomes more democratic; if we succeed in getting a clear political programme, a socialist programme; if our leaders become accountable so that if they don't implement that programme they can be replaced, then I think our chances are good because society is in a crisis, we don't operate in a vacuum. Capitalism is going through a period more like the twenties and thirties than the fifties and sixties and I don't believe the next ten or twenty years will be very happy ones for ordinary people, unlike the fifties when things appeared to get better all the time. Just because of that large numbers of people who until now have seen political action as a luxury are going to be forced to see it as a necessity to defend what has been won over the years let alone to extend those gains. In that sense I'm optimistic because I think that if the Labour Party reflects the political aspirations of its rank and file (and I think it must do eventually or it will split), then the future is ours. We shall see an enormous revulsion against the Tories and their policies and against the kind of society they stand for and this will bring about a far more radical Labour Government than any we've seen until now; whether it will be a Labour Government with the courage and the clarity of programme to make fundamental changes I don't know. I've not got a crystal ball but I think we shall have the *opportunity* to bring about socialism in this country in the foreseeable future – in the next ten or fifteen years – but nothing is inevitable. If we failed society could collapse like the Roman Empire but this time there wouldn't be much left. In that sense it's a case of socialism or annihilation and I think we shall have the opportunity, yes, I do.

I don't see an immediate threat of nuclear war. Capitalists are not all that stupid, the thing about nuclear weapons is that there isn't anyone left to pick up the pieces afterwards so it wouldn't be a very sensible way of maintaining your society and your profits. But imagine a situation like the nineteen thirties in Germany; suppose the Labour movement had failed and the unemployed and the middle classes began to despair, began to look round for some strong man; imagine this sort of thing happening in a country like America, say, and an equivalent of Hitler coming to power, under those circumstances nuclear war would be possible. That's what could happen if we fail to

94

change society; I suppose that's why I'm an activist — I've got a child! I want to be sure that there's a future for my children.

As for racialism, those prejudices are bound to exist in a country like this; we've got an imperialist past. I lived in Brixton for some time and there were poor white people as well as poor black people. Who stood for them? Nobody. No jobs. They had their houses burgled all the time because there were so many kids without work they went round burgling everyone; they couldn't see any hope in life. So — these blacks weren't here before — things have got like this because of these blacks. Vicious prejudices. But you can attack it so long as you're willing to take up the social issues. You get nowhere by saying love your neighbour. Admirable sentiment but the reply you get from Brixton is — you come and live here, you living in posh houses at the other end of London. We're living next to them, if people make a noise we hear it because the walls are thin; schools are overcrowded and bad and its our children who suffer; everyone's unemployed and there's crime, we're the victims. Don't tell us to love our neighbours unless you can offer solutions to the problems. That's the criticism I have of the leaders of our movement; they make enchanting noises about racialism but when it counts they've succumbed to the pressures themselves — immigration controls, for heaven's sake; if that's not accepting the argument that the problems are due to too many people coming in I don't know what is. Again, if you're not willing to stand for your ideas and fight for your ideas you've only yourself to blame if the muck of racialism gains ground. When the Labour movement has taken up the issue it has drained away a bit, for instance in the last year or so when people have really tackled the issue of the National Front; they've lost a lot of ground. That's how I see it. In Sheffield it's not such a problem because we've got a very strong Labour movement but in Rotherham for instance where Labour is not so strong and active there is a problem. It's significant that it's there that the National Front have concentrated their activities.

GOVINDASWAMY SELVARAJAN

55. Born in Madras, India. Has lived
in England since 1955. Known as 'Selva'.

When I was 13 I was active in the Indian Nationalist Youth League, shouting slogans and marching and working for the election of local candidates and having debates about freedom. We had a great South Indian poet Subranya Bharathi who inspired us and in 1942 I was sent to jail. Later on I led a textile strike and by this time I was a Trotskyist. I was released from jail on the day of Independence and became a member of the Central Committee of the Bolshevik Leninist Party of India which is Trotskyist and was the youngest member of the Committee at that time. They joined the Socialist Party of India in 1949 which I thought was a betrayal and left them. I was right for it all came to nothing.

In 1955 I came to England for personal reasons for one year and I have stayed here ever since. First I worked in a televison factory, later I became Warden of the Indian Student Bureau and after that I became a teacher at the suggestion of Donald Chesworth who was a member of the London County Council at that time. There was a shortage of teachers in mathematics and physics and they were eager that I should join. I had two degrees, a Master's degree in physics and my law degree – I had practised in India for about five years as a lawyer.

I took a close interest in the Asian Socialist Fellowship with Kenneth Younger. It was quite left wing in those days and I became a member of the Militant Group and played an active part – I was on the editorial board of the paper until I decided to leave them in 1960. I came to Putney in 1961 and married. My wife has recently graduated and is now studying for another degree.

I undertook a political tour of Europe and was travelling from Denmark to Norway by motorcycle when I had a serious accident and cracked my skull. I was incapacitated for a long time and it was not until 1965 that I joined the Putney Labour Party. I soon became a member of the General Management Committee but the Chairman at that time was an Irish bloke who used to get the creeps as soon as I stood up and would always try to stop me talking. At that time there were members of various socialist groups on the GMC but I did not belong to any of them. I was quite happy on the GMC in those days for other Chairmen used to give me a fair crack of the whip but the

Chairman of my local ward often used to try to shut me up but she did not often succeed.

In 1968 I was invited to join the candidates' list for the Borough Council Elections but none of the Putney wards wanted me. I went outside Putney to a ward elsewhere in Wandsworth but the meeting was packed with relatives of the candidates and I was defeated by one vote. Eventually I was chosen in Nightingale Ward but they decided not to fight it. Without telling me I was sent canvassing in another ward and it was only when I looked at the election address that I realised that I was not canvassing for myself!

In 1977 I was elected delegate to the Annual Conference of the party and spoke at that Brighton Conference. About then the wards were reorganised and Putney was split into East and West. I was in East Putney but I knew none of my new colleagues and they did not renew my membership of the GMC but chose others. I have not been very active since then. When I was at Conference I went to a meeting of the Campaign for Labour Party Democracy but they did not allow me to speak.

When Ian McGarry was Agent he was concerned to get work done and would accommodate the left and the right in order to achieve that. So the GMC was always very democratic but the ward varied from year to year. Very few people from Putney went on the Annual May Day March, one year it was the two McGarrys, Kevin Walsh and myself. Nowadays the Militant Group is much more active within the party. If you want to get your views taken seriously you must be active within the party.

I have never received any promotion in my job with the ILEA. As you know I believe this to be due to racial prejudice and as my MP you tried, without ultimate success, to do something about it. However, I must be one of the few teachers to have had his individual complaint aired in the House of Commons, especially a complaint against the Race Relations Board which I took to the Court of Appeal. My job is very low level but I keep in touch with advanced physics privately. Occasionally I felt that there was colour prejudice against me in the Putney Labour Party but, on the other hand, there were times when I felt that I influenced the party in a leftward direction. By the way, I think you commanded a high personal vote in Putney and but for that we should have lost the seat well before 1979.

DAVID GRUGEON

From 1962 to 1965 I was Borough Councillor for the West Hill Ward
here in Putney. This was an accident, in that Ratepayers stood against
Conservatives and let three Labour Councillors in. I was involved in
some early plans for the Open University and worked with Michael
Young and Brian Jackson who founded the National Extension College
in 1963. The year before I had met Richard Hoggart in Leicester
where he lived. I was very young at the time but I learned from him
that if you're in on something you don't give up at the first success.
For example, Richard Hoggart had been a member of the Albermarle
Committee on Youth Services and when it produced its report he was
still going regularly to London, keeping in touch with civil servants on
the further stages of implementation of the recommendations of the
report. So I saw that if you do a lot of work for a particular goal, like
the publication of a report or the election of the first Labour MP for
Putney, you don't give up at that point, that's only the beginning.

So we had to say OK, we've won Putney against all the odds (I
remember the night you were elected, people still had that ancient
sort of death wish, they couldn't believe it and so I whispered in their
ears 'Putney! Isn't that the place where they have the Boat Race?')
and so we've broken the tradition but we still have to hold it and to do
that and for 15 years was remarkable and would not have been
achieved if we had not maintained the commitment. Indeed, we had to
go further towards involving people, informing them and consulting
them about the political developments they hoped to see and how to
keep in touch with their MP and with their Councillors and so on. One
of the things that helped us was that we had a large membership of the
Labour Party, partly due to the work of Anne Kerr who built up a
big membership in the late fifties in the Roehampton London County
Council estates. We had ,3,500 members in Putney which, was quite
phenomenal at that time. There was no sympathetic local press and we
had to do something to fill that gap so we ran a monthly magazine of
our own called *WHY?* This was in imitation of *Which?* which, as
everyone knows has been very successful and there was another one on
the educational scene called *Where?* (both started by Michael Young).
As ours was on politics we thought it a good idea to call it *WHY?* and we
badgered people from different parts of the constituency and from
different standpoints to write for it on everything from nursery

schooling to national politics and, of course, you wrote a regular parliamentary piece on the problems of a party with a majority of three or four.

I got married in 1968 and we settled in Battersea. I was teaching in a teachers' training college having previously been a primary school teacher and I was also doing broadcasting for adult correspondence students. As soon as the Open University started I applied and was lucky enough to get a job looking after the whole of the East Anglian region so that took us to Cambridge in 1969 and so we were quite taken away from Wandsworth and Putney. I was also too occupied earlier to remain a member of the Borough Council and so did not seek re-election in 1965.

Since then I've known a number of Labour parties. A common feature is the incredible diversity of people who belong to the Labour Party wherever I've been, whether in Cambridge or Bedford or in the rural areas. The difference in Putney was the sheer amount of political activity, the high level of discussion, the carrying of that discussion to the doorstep and going out on much more recruitment and surgery work and suchlike activities. We always knew that Putney was marginal although it took a long time to persuade Transport House of that. The difference was quite marked on election days. Over the last 20 years I've probably been in twenty different constituencies helping at various parliamentary council and by-elections. In most local committee rooms it was a case of nothing but tea and biscuits until the afternoon and then leave it until the children are home from school and then leave it until after tea and so it goes on. I never experienced that in Putney, it was the only place I encountered where the machine was worked properly and three knockups was the regular thing. Putney was the only place I've ever been in where you not only knocked up once but went back and back and back until you knew they'd been to vote. That was only one small example of the degree of efficiency which was normal in Putney.

When you move about the country and change jobs and have children it is easy to drop your commitment to the Labour Party right down the scale but someone usually comes round and that's how you start working again. If no one comes round, that's how people drop out. In Putney when new housing estates went up we went in there in the first month and picked up their membership while it was fresh. In other parties I've been in they'd say let them settle in for a bit but by then it's too late and they've got used to the idea of not being a member. There are always the Liberals who have nothing to do in life but get involved in the local community by picking up the dogshit before it's been dropped and if you're not careful they get it first.

My wife and I have a continuous moral commitment to the Labour Party which means a continuous feeling of guilt that we haven't done enough. We've gone to ward meetings, we've been Ward Chairman, Treasurer, Membership Officer and so on. Now the children are at school my wife has become a JP and has stood for the District Council and I was elected to the Bedford County Council at a by-election. I'll soon be back to the 500 hours a year which was reckoned to be the proper stint of an active member of the Putney Labour Party. One probably has to accept that in peoples' life and work cycles there will be quiescent times and active times but it is crucial to maintain the link and to be ready when people are ready themselves to come back into full activity.

How did you first become a socialist?

I was paid for by the Labour London County Council for boarding and tuition as a boy. I was at a school outside London for seven years and while I was there I used the local public library regularly. It had a full range of newspapers including the *Daily Worker* as it then was which I should never have seen at the boarding school which took only the more respectable rags such as the *Express* and the *Mail* and other such rubbish. There I discovered the *Manchester Guardian* as it then was and started to read Alternative Viewpoint in that paper. When I was younger I think I felt that educated people were mostly small c or big C Conservatives; they might be a bit thick but could be trusted to act honourably and rationally and do their best for the world, etc. Two or three things happened to knock that image. One was the hanging of Ruth Ellis. It seemed quite extraordinary to me that we should hang a woman who would not have been hanged in France because her crime would have been regarded as a *crime passionel*. It was quite shattering to me that someone's life should be taken on such a basis. The second thing was Suez. To read an editorial in the *Guardian* which said something to the effect that 'this is an act of provocation without any justification except possibly that of brief expediency' and soon after to learn that there was not even that justification, this literally kept me awake for hours on end, night after night, because my whole world was overturned; my assumption that people would act honourably and decently was swept away and I realised that we had in power not merely well-intentioned cretins but people who were not even well-intentioned and were not honest or honourable. The whole experience moved me very strongly towards disarmament. I read Fenner Brockway's autobiography and books by Clement Attlee and others and I moved temporarily into a Lib/Lab position until the 1959 election when I was so shocked by the re-election of the party which had perpetrated Suez on the scandalously materialistic cry of 'You've Never Had it So Good', that I became wholeheartedly Labour which I saw was the only party likely to win power and to be able to act honourably in terms of democracy and our position in the world in relation to developing countries and all the other decent objectives of a young man who was trying to make rational sense of society.

I joined the Young Socialists in Putney although I was in the middle of my undergraduate course in Cambridge because I felt it essential to maintain local links in my home community and I was contemptuous of academic socialists who were not prepared to get their hands dirty and join in local constituency politics.

Were you born in Putney?

No, in Brixton. We were bombed out and I was evacuated during the war, when, incidentally, I met Jomo Kenyatta, and later we bought a house in Southfields where my mother still lives. My parents were middle-class, certainly not Labour supporters, though my father was brought up very rigidly among Plymouth Brethren, his father was a bank manager in Kent and my mother's father was an accountant in a milling firm in Newport. I remember when I was eleven years old going down the road to pick up a poster supporting Churchill and I joined something called the 'vile vermin' which was supposed to be the Conservatives' answer to Aneurin Bevan. It was a surprise to me to learn much later than my parents had voted Liberal in 1945. I just assumed they had been Conservative.

What do you recall about your period on the Wandsworth Borough Council?

I was one of the youngest members of the Council having been elected in 1962 when I was 23. It seemed to me important to give back something for having received so much public money first in being sent to boarding school and later to university. It was a painful experience in many ways. The Labour Party had been out of office for twelve years. There was an old guard which had been trained by the majority Conservatives in such habits as hanging on to their aldermanic gowns and they did not like the new brash youngsters coming in and telling them that all this was rubbish and that the people of Wandsworth would not thank them for going round in that kind of braided rhubarb. They were taken aback but they clung on to the chairman-ships and to many of the old formalities. It was a difficult time, both for them and for us. Very few of the new intake had worked in committee or knew how to present arguments and we had to learn as we went along. One found that odd events occurred. Senior officials of the Council would talk to developers about pulling down parts of the Borough and putting up some great office and commercial buildings. Fortunately, some of the new intake knew their way about and were able to recognise a rip-off when they saw one. They advised that the Council should not fall for the line which was being peddled, for the return in Council flats which was being offered was trifling in comparison with the benefits conferred on the developer. I remember making 21 'phone calls in one weekend to members of the Labour Group on the Council to ensure that they did not take at face value the line they were being sold by the old guard backed by the officers. That kind of activity was frenetic and one felt that hundreds of hours were being spent simply resisting the dominant ethos of the Council which had been brought over from the previous Conservative administration.

It was delightful to discover in later years that the new broom which we represented really came to power in Wandsworth and stood up for Labour policy and did not fall for the old smooth ways which had let the people of Wandsworth down for so many years.

On the other hand, one could work with the brighter members of the old guard. I remember old George Rowe when he was being made Mayor. You were supposed to make nostalgic references to glorious occasions in Wandsworth's past and George referred to the funeral of King George V. Everyone was ready for a good old sentimental memory when old George said, 'I remember the day well. I was collecting horse manure at the time.'

While I was a member of the Borough Council I was also a member of all sorts of protest groups, the Campaign for Nuclear Disarmament, the Campaign for Comprehensive Education, there was a tide at the time and in the Council Wandsworth was missing it. It was good training in knocking your head against a brick wall but it cooled me off local government work for a long time. It is only now, coming on to the Bedfordshire County Council, that I feel able to put that experience to good use.

What is your job now?

I am still with the Open University. Now I live in Bedford and work from the Open University HQ at Milton Keynes. I am still concerned with our unique developments in the regions but nowadays I help to coordinate this side of our activity from the university itself. The Open

University is probably the only very large-scale distance teaching organisation in the world which has been able to build in an economical but highly necessary and successful support service in the localities.

What do you feel about the present political scene?

It's a bit like 1959. An incredibly selfish and hypocritical prospectus was sold and in practice it has revived the basic arguments for socialism in this country. It is carrying out an extraordinary amount of political education daily. Members of the Labour Party now have the opportunity of making the tenets of socialism come alive. Like last week's photo in the *Bedfordshire Times* of a lobby outside County Hall, with my two children holding up a poster to save our schools and my wife being interviewed on the price of school meals and the size of classes. People are being hit where it hurts and we now have every chance of showing that this extremist government could be the last Conservative Government in this country and that's what gives me courage in a time of great depression.

28. Solicitor. Active in the Labour Party since his teens. Single.

I remember being given masses of leaflets to deliver during the 1964 general election when I was thirteen. I helped again in the 1966 election by which time I was actually a member of the party. At this time, however, most of my activity was turned towards the Campaign for Nuclear Disarmament rather than the Labour Party. A little later on I became involved in a by-election for the local County Council in Petersfield where we lived and soon after that I found myself Secretary of the Petersfield Labour Party for a couple of years until I moved to London. I lived for a few months in Fulham and then moved to Putney where I've lived ever since. I qualified as a solicitor in 1974.

The Putney Labour Party made a great impression on me; Petersfield was very small and the part of Fulham I was in was completely inactive from the Labour point of view. I was never at ease in Fulham where there appeared to be a lot of squabbling while Putney was united on a broad left basis and differences of view did not degenerate into hostility. Putney's organisation was also much better. Rows in Putney were not over major issues but on such matters as the parking scheme. I was personally against fighting the Euro-elections but since they decided to participate I think the Putney Party adopted the right policy of playing these bogus elections down.

I am now Secretary of the Thamesfield Ward where I live and am on the General Management Committee of the party. I was Membership Secretary of the party for more than two years. I think everyone needs an interest outside their work and my interest happens to be politics; others may be more concerned with sport or the arts but I've long had this interest in politics and the best way to show that interest and to develop it is to be active in the Labour Party. Many people with a political interest these days often concern themselves with particular causes but I think you can have much more influence within a political party.

Most of the time I find political activity fulfilling; for example, when we controlled the Borough Council, ordinary members of the party could have direct discussions with Labour Councillors involved in decision-making. Councillors in Putney in my experience took notice of the views of active members of the party. Of course, ordinary party work can be very humdrum and it is important that each meeting shall contain some political content. There's no quicker way to kill a party than to confine discussion to minor administrative questions about who is going to run which stall at the bazaar. At ward meetings in Putney we nearly always have a speaker and the GMC discusses resolutions at most meetings. When I was at Petersfield the branches never bothered to send in resolutions for discussion. When you were MP the rank and file member could even get at the government and certainly at Parliament so you begin to establish a chain of accountability. Trade union members who are not active in the party and only pay the political levy often don't think of themselves as Labour Party members and do not play the same role as an active individual member. It is rather farcical that these votes count the same at Party Conference. Something needs to be done about the Labour Party's internal democracy. One way of improving matters might be to split up the block vote so that the unions vote according to regions and sections rather than as a whole; that would be more democratic but I recognise the difficulties in bringing such changes about. I fear the possibility of a move to the right among the trade unions. If that occurred it might encourage the authoritarian tendencies among the leadership of the party.

It has always been my motive in politics to help to bring about change to the benefit of the community; change for socialism. I was a candidate in a hopeless Tory seat — Gosport — at the last general election; I was adopted early so that there was a long run-up period which became tedious at times but I enjoyed constituency activities, going to Party Conference and the campaign itself. I am undecided whether to stand again but I probably will seek some sort of elected office whether it be Council, GLC or Parliament. I was on the Council Labour Group for two years as a representative of the Local Government Committee and I have seen, even at that level, the dangers of elected representatives becoming divorced from the local party. I think the local party represents the local community, and Labour voters especially, to a much greater extent than is generally thought. The opinions of the community make themselves heard through the local party and I think that when we controlled the local Council at times we did lose touch; for example in raising the rate too high immediately prior to the Council elections which we lost, partly as a result.

The last Labour Government fell for the same cause — failure to keep in touch with our own people. Perhaps surprisingly, the National Executive of the party seems to me to be very good at sensing the feelings of the party and the government of the day ignores it at its peril. It should have much more influence; for example, the Cabinet should never write the party manifesto. A Labour Government should differ much more from the Tories in the way it runs the economy than has been the case recently. I want to see a full-blown socialist party put into operation as soon as possible. We need to control the economy and not hand it over to market forces.

The most worrying thing for us is the way our total vote and our share of the vote has declined in recent general elections — down to less than 40 per cent of the vote; if that was to go on we could be condemned to permanent opposition. We've got to become a more dynamic and idealistic party if we are to get these votes back; we must have a really progressive manifesto, not one like the last which said 'Look how good we've done', when it was painfully obvious we hadn't done all that well. Next time we must put socialist policies into practice.

MRS PHYLLIS COURTNEY

Aged 55. Married to Peter Courtney. Three
sons. All now married and away
from home.

We came to live in Putney in 1956 but did not join the Labour Party
until 1965. Both of us were Labour voters but with a young family
we could not be active in politics. When we felt the children were old
enough we tried to join the party but found it quite difficult. We saw
members and said we would like to join; nothing happened, but after
you were elected to Parliament we became quite determined. We got in
touch with the Agent, then Ian McGarry, paid our subscriptions and
almost at once were taken up into the party and became active. Peter
had already known Ian and Christine through the CND movement, he'd
met them on marches and we joined Thamesfield Ward which at that
time only had six active members so they were very glad to see us.

Peter was soon on the General Management Committee and
enjoying it very much and I followed a year or two after. All of us
played an active part in the campaign against the war in Vietnam. Both
of us came from Labour-supporting families although none were
politically active. My father was a taxi-driver and in those days they
were very poor sometimes earning only a few shillings in a day. Putney
was famous in the CND movement for being one of the constituency
parties which gave full support and that made us keen to join.

Soon after joining I became involved in the Women's Section. That
folded up some years ago; we found many of the younger women who
joined the party refused to come into the Women's Section because
they felt it unsuitable for a liberated female to belong to a special
section, after all, there wasn't a men's section; they felt you should get
involved in your ward as the men did. On the other hand, in the
Women's Section we regretted this because we found there were
women who were too nervous to attend a ward meeting and although
they might join, played no active part at all. We got some of these
women to attend a Women's Section meeting in someone's home and
several of them afterwards became very active party members having
built up their confidence; we did a lot of political education, much
more than was done at ward level at that time.

In earlier days I was tied up with the family and Peter was the more
politically active; he was already reading politics even before we joined

the party. We've both been invited to stand for the Council but we always refused; we're interested in national politics and we wanted to continue to work in the party. Once you get on to the Council it takes up all your free time and there's no time for party work, or not as much. We felt that there should be some people who gave the party their first priority. When leading members of the party got on the Council we lost a certain amount of impetus on national issues. We had a successful Labour Council and obviously we wanted that but we *did* lose sight of national issues for a while. If you're not careful meetings can degenerate into questions of paving stones; housing and social services are important but you mustn't forget that the Labour Party is concerned with national and even international questions.

We've had lots of disappointments on these matters but we've always felt, always known, that the Labour Party holds the only possible answer for us and for the country, so it would be quite unthinkable to stand back. Before we got involved in the Labour Party we did have a look at the Liberal Party but we soon decided it was not for us because we look ahead for socialism and however disappointing it is at times, over the years we've made such headway that we've changed the terms in which politics are discussed. People know what Labour Government is like and they're already getting restless with the Tories; they expect what Labour offers and they won't like losing the benefits of Labour Government either nationally or locally. So, however slowly, we make progress. I remember Michael Foot saying much the same to one of our Annual General Meetings. We've been fed up but never to the point when we even thought of not taking an active part. On the contrary, we've tried to do a bit more.

We do a lot of drudgery but find that the political activists are always willing to lend a hand at fund-raising and so on. It's often difficult to get people to take responsibility before an event but on the day of a jumble sale or whatever, they rally round however much they moan and complain. There are irksome tasks to be done but someone has to do them.

My three sons are all Labour supporters and two of them quite active. My eldest son is a director of Rye Express which does printing for community groups and Labour parties. My daughter-in-law is on the GMC of another constituency Labour party, not such a progressive one as Putney. She often envies us and goes back to her party saying why don't you do this or that, such as having tenants' representatives attending the Council and so on.

I don't think that people like Peter and myself have a direct influence on the course of events but I think we do influence the way others think and behave and that the Putney Labour Party as a whole has done this. We have done a lot of canvassing over the years and we've seen people come round and eventually join the party and a few become active members. People wonder why you work for the Labour Party and they become more conscious of it and begin to think in a more social and less selfish way.

Even when I was quite young there were discussions in our home about why we should vote for a Labour Government. My mother who'd come from a country farming background in Gloucestershire was not so sure that it was quite the right thing to do; where she came from they voted Tory and did as they were told so we had arguments but Labour won them.

I was the first woman to chair the Putney Labour Party in 1972/3 and at that time we were campaigning successfully against the motorway so perhaps you could say that sometimes I made more direct and personal attempts to influence the course of events and have even done so with the help of many others. That motorway would have divided Putney and destroyed it and we worked really hard to stop it. We are still hoping against hope that we shall be able to stop them from pulling down the small shops in Lacy Road. In addition to these local efforts Peter and I have often gone on national demonstrations, anti-apartheid, Chile and so on; we like to be there with all the people.

Until I decided to retire early, quite recently, I was a part-time civil servant in the Ministry of Defence but I never allowed this to interfere with my political activities. Peter too has always succeeded in keeping his business life in insurance and his personal and political life quite separate although obviously it has affected our approach to work.

Older people, like you and Marie and Peter and I, find no difficulty in working together in politics but I think membership of the Council puts marriages with young children under great strain. Wives can feel very cut off when their husbands spend every night at the Town Hall but nowadays marriage itself is going through a difficult period and it may have nothing to do with the Council although we've had several break-ups; these marriages would perhaps have broken up anyway for other reasons.

The Labour Party has become a large part of our lives at 14 Abbotstone Road. As you know our house was the only HQ the Labour Party had after selling 168 Upper Richmond Road and it took years to move into the present place. We got our inspiration from the Putney Labour Party, from it being a left-wing party, you were the

MP and Ian was the Agent and it was exciting that Putney of all places
should go left. Ian McGarry had the rare ability to inspire people into
working for the party and so he was a valuable asset. After Ian left I
became Secretary of the party as a volunteer for eighteen months
and as I was working part-time as well, that was a period of
exceptionally hard work. I had a lot of help from Peter and others
or I could not have done it.

To be involved in politics, to be committed to it, is to have
wider horizons than yourself and your immediate family; if you
become conscious of how the rest of the world is living you cannot
live for yourself alone. But you must also enjoy it. Peter and I
enjoy political activity immensely. We could not live properly
without it and our lives are now bound up with the party. I remember
when Ian McGarry first asked me to go canvassing I felt quite sick.
I dreaded it but after I'd done it a few times I was astonished to find
I was really enjoying it. People are generally so pleasant.

I'm glad to see younger people getting on to the General
Management Committee but sorry that some of the older ones are
dropping out. We want to keep a good age range in the party. On the
other hand the balance between men and women is still very good in
Putney, there's no sex discrimination here and never has been in
my time.

*Married to another active member of
the Labour Party. Two young children.
Leader of the Labour Party Housing Group on
the Borough Council. Family lives in
a Greater London Council house in
Roehampton.*

In 1959 I came up to London to work in the civil service and lived in
Putney quite by chance. There was little work in the West Country and
I became a tax-gatherer in the Inland Revenue. I am still in taxation
work but for a large private company. I married in Putney in 1965
having met my wife in the civil service hostel I was staying in at the
time.

I came from a Labour family but did not join myself until 1967
when I decided that the party in government was deserting the likes of
me and other working-class people so I thought it was time to make a
personal contribution. I attended ward meetings and was soon on the
General Management Committee. I have missed very few meetings
since then. In 1971 I was elected to the Council.

There were three levels of activity within the party and still are.
There were those who were just members and seldom played any
active role; there were those who turned up at meetings and helped the
work of the party, good solid folk with a great disparity of opinions,
and within them a smaller group who talked politics to each other in
pubs and everywhere else and who gave the party a good feeling, a good
atmosphere. They tended to surround Ian McGarry but they were not an
exclusive group; anyone could join in and the membership has changed
almost 100 per cent in my time; they were and are like-minded people
but never a clique; a mixed group of 30 to 50 people who were
political friends and continued to talk politics to each other outside the
formal framework of official meetings. Ian McGarry, and not only
because of his political ability, had the knack of attracting people and
keeping them active.

After 1971 I became more and more absorbed in Council work and
have never missed a meeting of the Council or of the Housing
Committee. Nearly all of us were both new and young; at 31 I was
about the average age, most of us had no experience of Council work
but Ian McGarry was elected Leader and in a short time we felt like

veterans. We had a very difficult time over the Tory Housing Finance Act in 1973. There was a major political row inside our group over the resistance of some of us to the implementation by Wandsworth Council of what was, by then, the law. Many of us felt that the interests of the families we represented demanded that we refuse to implement this highly objectionable and anti-working-class piece of legislation. There were other members of the group who said that the law is the law and we must obey it. They won; we lost. At the time it was bitter and acrimonious but looking back over the years one can see that it did us an awful lot of good because it brought out fundamental arguments on why we were there and what we were supposed to be about. I've never felt any regrets at all and I think other members may feel the same. Ian McGarry resigned as Leader and some other office-holders went with him but the contrast between him and his successor was so great that soon people who had voted against him were asking him to come back. There was further misunderstanding about the terms on which this was done. I thought the return was unconditional but Ian believed that he was accepting a proviso that the Act be implemented and acted accordingly. There was further acrimony and when the next round of rent increases came, eight of us still voted against. However, after a month or so of bitterness we dropped it because we could see the benefits of having a decent leadership again.

The Council occupied so much of my time that I was not able to be as active in the party on other matters as I should have liked; instead of instigating discussion myself or framing resolutions to go to the GMC from the ward, I tended to take part in discussions proposed by others. For example, I would have liked to bring up the problem of the relationship between a Labour Government and the trade unions and I think we should have spent much more time on Northern Ireland but there was simply no time to give my mind to preparing the ground.

The GMC has become much more middle-class in recent years but this does not seem to have affected policy very much; more seriously we have lost a number of fiery and passionate personalities who have moved out of the district. These people would always want to take major political issues by the throat; recently there has been a decline in the quality of discussion and in the quality of the resolutions before the GMC. Nowadays the GMC only seems to get excited about such irrelevant issues as the Putney parking scheme. We've lost some politically committed people who argued forcefully on the real issues; Putney has a fairly mobile population and the active membership of the party turns over quite quickly. Who knows maybe next month we shall be joined by some firebrands!

In 1974 I was the party delegate to Annual Conference but this was just a jamboree between elections and not a proper conference at all so I hope to go again one day.

Your wife is also active in the Putney Party; does this present problems?

I spend a lot of time on the Putney Party and the Wandsworth Borough Council. My wife has agreed that she will be responsible for looking after the children or seeing that there is someone else to do so and this means that she has deliberately taken a back seat for a number of years now. She's very keen and will become more active but for now there is a limit to what the two of us can do.

What about the current political scene?

Like many other active members of the party I would like to see more democracy within the Labour Party; to see the National Executive more powerful and some participation by constituency parties in such matters as electing the Leader. All the same this is not an opportune time to become obsessed with the matter. What is most crucial now is that we get together with our supporters; that we look after their interests and they know it; that we explain to them what is going on, the consequences of attacks on the public services and so on. We are in danger of losing that wide unquestioning support which we've enjoyed ever since the war and it is time we repaid that support from folk who through good times and bad have voted Labour so solidly. The way to do it is to explain to our own supporters and to demonstrate to them that the Labour Party is there to look after their interests. We must defend their standards of living at all points and be seen to do so; we must trim the worst excesses of Tory Government both nationally and locally. We must explain what is being done, why the Tories are doing it and what the Labour Party is doing now and will be doing in future. In Putney we are already getting that message across in housing by participation and discussion with tenants' associations. When we were in power we set up a system under which representatives of the tenants regularly met with the Council to tell us what they thought we should be doing. The tenants now know that they have a voice and it is now being used by tenants' representatives to oppose Tory housing policies in the Borough. They are now telling the Tories where they are going wrong; they have learned and are learning the facts of political life and the message goes back to the tenants on the estates. There is now developing a grass roots campaign against the reality of Tory Council policies and there is a close association between the remaining Labour members on the Council and the tenants' associations. As things get more difficult people will increasingly turn back to the Labour Party. Constituency parties have the job of seeing that supporters of our party become well informed on national affairs as well; also on what the Labour Party is doing and why. Even when the party is not in power it must still be willing to assist individuals and groups in their battles against authority. If the party is seen to be doing that it will be remembered at election time. People are confused and perplexed by what they read in the papers where everything is personalised as a struggle between Callaghan and Benn.

Have you thought of becoming an MP yourself?

Not seriously, no. It's not excluded but I have enough on my plate as it is without bothering about that. For example, I'm worried about the relationship between the Labour Party and the trade union movement. Without the trade unions the party would not exist but a new generation of leaders has not yet made the impact of the Jack Joneses and Hugh Scanlons and this may show itself in the Labour Party by a move to the right. This may be arrested by the development of a major struggle between the trade unions and the Tory Government. When I look back I think of the 1970 general election in Putney; it was wonderful to hold this constituency against the Tory tide at that time. There was a magnificent atmosphere here in those days, a great campaign, nothing was too much trouble, we did an incredible amount of work and everything went well for us. We rose to a great peak with a tremendous rally in Roehampton; those people wanted Hugh Jenkins to be elected, they wanted it desperately in spite of their disappointment with the Labour Government. After that peak we won Wandsworth Borough Council but the sad thing was that the party became less dynamic because 15 leading members of the Putney Labour Party became Councillors and their efforts necessarily became more dispersed. Now we've had a crushing defeat and it's time to concentrate on re-building the party and widening its influence.

CYNTHIA ROBERTS

*43. Married to Denis Roberts, professional
photographer, also a member of the Labour
Party. They live with their two children in
a GLC maisonette off the Alton Estate,
Roehampton.*

I was born in Maidstone in Kent where I lived for the first 20 years of
my life. My family were strong supporters of the Labour Party. I
remember being taken to the Working Mens' Club when I was about
nine years old and having the basic differences between the
Conservative Party and the Labour Party explained to me.

Later I became a theological student. I completed the course and was
about to be placed in a parish when I met my husband. It was a choice
of going ahead with parish work or getting married and in the end my
husband won. We lived in Kensington in privately owned accommodation
but were evicted when the owner died and the GLC found us
accommodation in the old East Hill Estate in Wandsworth. It was a very
unhealthy and dilapidated place and we applied to leave for the sake of
our children's health and we ended up in our present place in Clarence
Lane. As you know, the East Hill Estate has since been pulled down.

My husband was already a member of the Labour Party. We came to
Clarence Lane in 1972, helped by Labour Councillor, Maria Marshall.
We arrived on May Day and were so grateful that we decided to devote
our spare energies to helping the Labour Party so as to help others in
our position. Quite apart from that, we realised that the Labour Party
stood for all the things we stood for. Soon after we joined, the
Secretaryship of the Roehampton Branch became vacant and I decided
to take it on and the more involved we became, the more interested we
became and we soon realised that our lives ran parallel with that of
the Labour Party and that was how it all started.

Both my husband and I soon got on to the General Management
Committee of the party. I served for a short while on the Local
Government Committee; I'm a school manager of Huntingfield School
and Vice-chairman of the Governors at Roehampton Gate School.
Politics began to take over our lives more and more. I thought of
standing for the local Council but Denis does not only work in the
day-time, he takes evening classes as well and I thought this would mean
too much evening work for a couple with young children. Also my own

115

development in politics was turning more and more into peace, security and foreign affairs, especially the Third World and disarmament and this could not be served by becoming a local councillor. We thought that if I became an MP Denis could give up his job teaching photography and would work with me and we would both devote all our working lives to the Labour Party. So I became a potential candidate on the 'B' list as they call it and soon after that I heard by chance that Eastleigh in Hampshire had had their candidate resign and were looking for a replacement. I was chosen there at a Selection Conference in June 1977. Of course, we did not win in that safe Tory seat but the Labour vote held up well in 1979 and since then I have become Secretary of Labour Action for Peace. The peace movement in this country has not been gaining ground in recent years and there is a big job to be done as the militarisation of Europe and the world is getting more and more serious. We have to find a way of bringing this home to people. When I talked to people about disarmament and peace their attitude was that my feet were not on the ground but when I spoke of defence and security their whole attitude changed. So I started to draw a distinct line between the Conservative Party's aggressive attacking strategy towards Eastern Europe and to contrast it with Labour's genuine defensive policy. When I started to do this and to draw attention to the prospects for peace through the Helsinki Final Act; that co-operation between Eastern and Western European states is growing; that the massive burden of defence expenditure is bankrupting this country; when I took that line people opened up and agreed that it is better to have a real defence policy than an attacking strategy.

I've learned a great deal from the Putney Labour Party. It is what I would call a fundamentally radical party; the General Management Committee is extremely well-informed and active. There is one activity I tried in Eastleigh which they might adopt and that is to carry out a public survey on particular topics. Say twice a year, to go out into the streets and collect opinions on a subject. Have three or four questions prepared and ask people what they think about them. Then you get a feeling of the attitude of people in different areas on various topics and you can weave that in with your own policies so that you present them in ways acceptable to people. I found this worked with the Common Agricultural Policy of the EEC. We have to get more of our own leaflets out to people as well and we have to bring people into our way of thinking and listen to what they have to say. We have to go out to the people more and draw them in.

I learned my basic socialism from the Putney Labour Party and I took enormous inspiration from the perseverance of our members when

116

the going was rough and I'm all in favour of more democracy in the party, they deserve it. We cannot have democratic socialism in this country without a thoroughly democratic party. The thing the Labour Party has suffered from appallingly in the past has been the patronage of the leadership. We must have a parliamentary Labour Party which carries out conference decisions in office and MPs must keep in touch with their General Management Committees. An MP is accountable to the basic principles of the party; he has a special relationship with his General Management Committee who are his advisory body and, of course, the MP has his accountability to the electorate as a whole. No MP should vote against a policy if his General Management Committee is in favour of it. Of course, you can't mandate an MP to the point of dotting the i's and crossing the t's but if he works closely with his officers there will be no problem. They will accept an occasional disagreement but cannot be expected to endure continual disagreement and hostility. I could never vote for the deployment and use of nuclear weapons and would always make this clear before selection. I could never vote to stay in the Common Market and would make this equally clear.

I've become closely involved in the area of peace and detente. I think the Helsinki Final Act is the way in which Europe should go. Co-operation between countries, the East and the West; if we have cultural, academic, educational, medical, scientific, technological exchanges together with commercial exchanges, the tension will be dramatically reduced. I want to see it reduced to the point at which NATO and the Warsaw Treaty Organisation are completely and concurrently phased out. I should like to see the development of research into means of neutralising nuclear attack rather than in preparing counter-attack. I should also like to see a UN peace-keeping force. I have made many other peace-orientated proposals to the Labour Party, based on our own Conference decisions including the running down of the Defence Sales Organisation.

If I am asked to contest a winnable seat I should be ready to become a Labour candidate again; it will depend on what I am advised to do and whether I am wanted.

One thing I would have great difficulty with is that question of abortion. With Putney, for example, that would be a problem for I cannot believe that abortion is the right way to deal with unwanted pregnancies for a foetus once conceived is a child, alive from about twelve weeks onwards. From my own experience I know that you can feel them move inside you. I feel strongly over all forms of killing people but I have had it pointed out to me that, of course, people with money will get abortions anyway and the whole problem is the back-street abortionist. This is a terrible problem for me and I don't know how I'm going to end up with it.

At 62 I suppose I'm one of the older members of the Putney Labour
Party. I had a rather unconventional early upbringing. I went to a
progressive school and learned to milk cows and a lot of economics
when other people were learning Latin. Eventually I went to Oxford
where I was deeply involved in Labour Party politics. I've had a
political background ever since I can remember; my mother was one of
those ladies to whom Mr Asquith used to write letters and he was the
father-figure of my childhood, my father having been killed in the
First World War. So I began with a strong Liberal background but I was
not allowed to go and meet Lloyd George when he came to stay
with the people next door — we were Asquithians.

But at the earliest possible opportunity, when I was 16, I joined the
Labour League of Youth and I've certainly been deeply committed to
Labour politics ever since.

My first job on leaving Oxford was with Lord Beaverbrook who
liked employing socialists. He asked me one question when I went to
see him for interview which was 'What are your politics?' I replied I was
right-wing Labour and he said that was as good as Conservative! I think
he was wrong but I've remained right-wing Labour.

Later on I became a political commentator with the BBC External
Services and, as the Corporation does not care for a real political
commitment on the part of its employees I wrote for *Socialist
Commentary* under the pseydonym of 'Catalpa', which is the Latin
name for the American bean tree; these are the trees which line New
Palace Yard and the idea was that I surveyed all the comings and goings
of Parliament.

I came to Putney in 1970 from Westminster where I had been a
member of the Labour Party and I was immediately involved in working
in that general election. At my first ward meeting in Putney I was
nominated for the General Committee and I've been a member ever
since. To begin with I found the GMC extremely unfriendly and it was
a long time before anybody on the Committee acknowledged that I
was a person at all. I found it extremely difficult to identify people on
the GMC — everyone was 'Trev' or 'Mike' or some abbreviation or
other, it was very confusing and it took me a long time to get my
bearings at all. As compared with most other members of the GMC I am
strongly on the right wing of the party so whether I am considered like

the drunk on a teetotal committee or the statutory woman among male chauvinists I don't know but there are a number of people there now who, regardless of politics, I have grown very fond of. I never quite know where the dividing line in politics comes, I remember when Jo Richardson came to address our Annual General Meeting last year I had prepared various arguments to throw at her about the alternative strategy and import controls and so on but in the event she talked about nothing but virginity tests on immigrants and, of course, we all agreed and were one happy party. There are so many things about which we agree, and yet so many we disagree about − I think I shall have to make a list and see where the real differences lie, and the more important unity.

I stood for the Council at the last Borough elections. I found it a most invigorating experience although I was almost at the bottom of the poll and I was enormously flattered to have been asked to stand. It would never have crossed my mind but Phyl Courtney said 'Why not put your name forward?' So I did and when I got on the short list I thought people must have taken leave of their senses.

I think some of the most unfriendly people have moved on and so perhaps I am not, on some issues, so out of step with the party as I once was. I don't think the Putney Party is quite as far left as it was when I first joined; perhaps the reverses we have had in Putney in the last two years have sobered people.

I was amazed that a branch of the party, not my own branch, sent my name forward for short-listing for the Euro-elections for I have never concealed the fact that I am at odds with the majority on being pro-EEC. My main criticism of the Putney Party would be that throughout the term of the last Labour Government − a minority government faced with every difficulty you can imagine − the party never seemed to have any inkling of what the government was up against; on the contrary the government was a main target for abuse and there seemed to be a failure to recognise that the real enemy was not the rest of the Labour Party but the Conservatives. I'm delighted to say that now that there is a Conservative Government in office I have no difficulty in supporting the resolutions which come up.

On local politics I think that Putney Labour Councillors were not sufficiently conscious that they had an electorate to face which might not approve of the way they had been running things. There was a tendency to see themselves in a vacuum and not in the context of politics at large where you have to face a critical electorate and an opposition which will do everything it can to do you down. The Tory Council which has followed them is almost too horrible; it seems to be out-Thatchering Thatcher in every way and the idea of their taking over the schools from the ILEA is totally ludicrous. They got in on the grounds that they would be able to cut rates or not raise them as much as Labour yet here they are proposing a scheme which would make the rates soar. They are asking to be thrown out.

As for the Putney Party now, well, one of our left-wingers agreed with me that the opportunity to smash into the Conservatives was lost at the 1979 Annual Conference so perhaps we are growing together. These arcane nigglings about the constitution are of importance but not to the watching world outside.

When did you first know that you were a socialist?

It was at the time of the 1929 election when I was twelve. I was at school and several naked young ladies were talking politics in the bathroom. One of them said 'Everyone in this country has enough to eat!' The complacency was unbearable. And I hit her! I realised that there was no future in the Liberal Party and since then I have been dedicated to the Labour Party. At about the same time the headmistress of my school announced one day that she was tired of superintending the education of the middle-class children and off she went to South Wales to teach the children of unemployed miners. She was a very remarkable lady and I recall a poem of hers: 'O modern world arise' there's a line in it – 'In labour and in love is hid the prize.'

I have a *hatred* of the British class system and a great enjoyment of equality when one comes across it. For example, when one has visited the Scandinavian countries which, I suppose, have as egalitarian a society as possible coupled with freedom, the way people look you straight in the face and everybody from the chambermaid in the hotel and the bus conductor are on terms of equality with you, I think this is such a liberating thing and the Labour Party is the only one which is committed to that conception of equality. I believe strongly in liberty but I don't believe you can have true liberty without true equality.

PETER HAIN

*Brought up in South Africa. Came to England
with parents in 1966 and soon nationally known
for activities against apartheid, particularly
in sport. Now Assistant Research Officer
with the Union of Post Office Workers.*

I joined the Young Liberals in the late sixties. At that time many of us
felt the Wilson Government was selling out on Vietnam, Rhodesia and
so on. With the growth of student politics at that time people were
looking for ways of stopping the rot. I joined the Young Liberals,
rather than the Labour Party, because they seemed to be doing
imaginative radical things. Over the years, however, I began to
appreciate the impossibility of shifting the Liberal Party into a
socialist and radical direction and I found this difficult to square with
my own political beliefs. Eventually I came to the position that if you
were serious about wanting to change things – if you were not a
dilettante of politics – then the Labour movement with all its warts, is
the only way. A number of young radicals who were active in such
pressure groups as the anti-apartheid movement reached the same
conclusion at about the same time. With some, it was a matter of
coming back into the Labour Party.

When I joined my first impression was of how different the Labour
Party is in reality from the media image of it. The media image is of a
party run by a cantankerous group of tightly knit Moscow-orientated
people of the far left; that simply is not true. In fact I found the left
within the Labour Party much weaker than I had expected from what
I had read and I feel there is a real need to strengthen it. There is a
certain amount of what you might call symbolic posturing; for example,
if you want to be respectable in the Labour Party you virtually have to
say you are 'of the left'; those are the opening few words to your
sentence before you expound your view. It becomes a cloak behind
which all sorts of confusions and problems have to be sorted out.

My second impression was of how much the major activity and
thinking of the party – its whole style – is geared towards elections,
Council or parliamentary. The party seems to have lost contact with its
own roots, not only through the failure of Labour Governments to
implement socialist policies but because the party itself has stopped
going out to people and involving people in political, and not only

electoral, activity.

I must add that I found the Labour Party very congenial. I was very grateful for the way in which I was welcomed, when it would have been understandable if there had been suspicion and antagonism given the circumstances in which I joined. That says a great deal for the Putney Party for it would have been understandable for them to have been sceptical of someone who had spent ten years in another party. I live in the Thamesfield Ward and the members included many young and active people and I felt I fitted in easily with them.

I've been to one Labour Annual Conference as the Party delegate — the 1970 one which was of course very exciting. I was impressed by the discussion of real issues and I found a sort of root passion there I had not seen at a party conference before. At the same time the procedure can be bureaucratic; it's a matter, once again, of re-building the bridges between party politics and the way most people react to them.

Your family were Liberals in South Africa?

Yes, I found Liberalism in Britain very different and never regarded myself as having really joined the Liberal Party here. You may remember that when I was President of the Young Liberals in Putney in 1970 we carried a resolution supporting your candidature rather than that of the Liberal candidate! I was never really comfortable in the British Liberal Party and when I left in September 1977 it was overdue. The Labour Party had adopted more radical positions, both on nationalisation and on workers' control. In addition the deterioration of the economy faced people with a stark choice: there could be no easy answer any more in single-issue politics nor in Young Liberal rhetoric; you had to decide where you stood on the major issues, such as unemployment and public expenditure. If I had been concerned with a political career it might have been better to stay a big fish in a small pond.

We left South Africa in 1966 when my father was denied a livelihood. My parents were both involved in opposition to apartheid and they were both banned. My father's banning order in 1964 contained a special provision which allowed him to communicate with his wife (and my mother had an addendum added to hers), as banned people are normally not allowed to communicate with each other! Soon after that an edict was issued to all architectural firms in Pretoria where we lived that if they employed my father (who is an architect) they would get no more public authority work. So we left because we had no choice and came to Putney where my parents are still active in the

Liberal Party.

In October 1975 I drove our car to W.H. Smith's to buy some typewriter ribbons. Unknown to me a thief had some minutes before, snatched £490 from Barclay's Bank in the Upper Richmond Rd. I parked on a yellow line outside Smith's — as it later turned out, right alongside four schoolboys who had joined the chase for this thief. He had run down Putney High Street, up Werter Road, thrown the money back at his pursuers and disappeared. Walking back these schoolboys apparently thought I was the thief, reported this to the police station and later, when I was having lunch at home, a whole lot of policemen arrived at the door. In spite of the fact that I could not have been guilty unless I was also a lunatic, I was nevertheless charged with the offence.

My face was known in Putney High Street as it was elsewhere at that time. Yet to have committed the theft, I would have had to rob a bank 300 yards from my home, to run down Putney High Street, to throw the money back, then to summon my car up from nowhere and to drive back and park alongside my erstwhile pursuers so they could have a good look at me! In spite of that ludicrous scenario, the charge was nevertheless proceeded with. The experience was both unpleasant and unreal; the police were simply not interested in the truth, they were determined to prosecute and the case raised important questions about police procedure. Fortunately one of the boys had disagreed with his friends that I looked like the thief and came forward as a defence witness. But once the other three had reported that it was me, there was then a prima facie case and it was difficult to stop the wheels rolling. Of course, I was aquitted, but the case revealed something badly wrong in the legal system. There were stories that I had been framed by the South African security people in this country and it is true that the thief (who was said to be my double) appeared to want to be seen. But then no one could have laid on four schoolboys, nor my decision to call on W.H. Smith at the right moment, so it seems improbable, though there have been assertions to the contrary by defecting South African agents. I have an open mind about it.

Do you want to be a Labour MP?

I wouldn't rule it out if people really wanted me to do it. But I feel temperamentally more comfortable operating outside the established political structures. If you want to bring about socialist change in this country, the missing dimension is and has been pressure from outside. I don't think you can bring about change solely by getting people elected to Councils and to Parliament. I don't see the failure of Labour

124

Governments in terms of them being baddies or corrupt or selling out — though there may have been elements of all of those things. I see it rather as the system entrapping the government, and, unless there is also change outside and pressure from outside, the effect of representatives can only be marginal. There must be a mood and a climate for socialism and I feel most happy in trying to make a contribution towards that.

When I was elected to the General Management Committee of the Putney Labour Party I was initially very impressed with the level of political discussion compared with the Liberals, but, as I got more involved, I found too much time being spent at the jumble sale level. I think we're swinging back to political discussion now. I was also struck by the failure of the Officers and Executive of the party to give a collective organisational lead. There is a lack of drive from the centre. It may be a post-Ian McGarry situation, missing a brilliant organiser and not realising that we must collectively replace him. We are inclined to agree things and expect them to be done instead of also agreeing on how they are to be done and who is to do what. This sometimes means that the same few willing workers — people like the Courtneys, Mike Williams and Judith Chegwidden — continue to carry the can.

On the other hand it seems to me that the Putney Labour Party has an accurate instinct which encourages it to reach the correct decisions on major issues. The party will always be on the side of the angels and there is no need to think twice. Putney's answer is always the radical socialist one, on economic issues, civil liberties, you name it, the democratic socialist answer is given pretty well every time.

Nevertheless, it is also the case that, to some extent, the party both locally and nationally has lost touch with its working-class base. It's no use saying that this is because we have not implemented socialist policies in government. That may well be part of the answer but we also have a real problem, in a hostile environment and in a time when working-class culture is being fragmented, we have a problem of going out to involve more of our own people on the estates and in the tenants' associations and especially the young people in our own concerns. We tried the latter with some success among young people in the Anti-Nazi League with our Rock Against Racism idea. We must not reject new political styles, for if we do not make an effort we shall become more and more representative of the left-wing professional middle classes rather than of our own mass base. Until we build up really active support outside the parliamentary structure, anything our representatives do inside the structure will be difficult and only partly effective. The pressures of socialist representatives, as you know better than I do, are such that unless you have really unstoppable pressure coming up from your own supporters, the task is almost impossible.

I see our task, not so much as that of getting the 'goodies' into Parliament or into the Cabinet, though that is important, but more in terms of re-building through the party a wider mass base for the struggle; a more socialist direction would be an automatic consequence of that development providing it is accompanied by widespread political discussion.

It might be necessary for people to be given more say in party decision-making, perhaps by an expanded General Management Committee and we should gradually move towards involving more and more people not only in the decision-making process, but in active campaigning. Activity holds the key to re-creating a mass Labour Party.

Since 1976 I have worked as Assistant Research Officer for the Union of Post Office Workers which has been a marvellous experience. It has also given me a working insight into the reality of trade unions about which there is a great deal of mythology not only in the media but from the left in the party too. For instance, advances such as the politicisation of the membership of public sector unions (e.g. NUPE, CSPA, SCPS, etc.) must be set against two other trends to which insufficient acknowledgement is given: first the absorption of the national trade union leadership on a corporatist basis and second the fact that recent wage militancy has encouraged an ethos of American-type trade unionism which is not linked to socialist struggle. In other words we must question the assumption that the undoubted increase in trade union strength *necessarily* strengthens the forces for socialism. We also need to give a greater priority to rank-and-file level activity and to building Labour Party workplace branches.

MARCIA DAVIES

*MA. Senior Lecturer
in Computer Studies at
South-West London College.*

I came to Putney soon after I left Southport to live and work in London and now I've lived here for thirteen years. After I graduated from Cambridge I went to work for ICI in Manchester. I was then transferred to London and eventually decided to teach here. My family was politically interested but my parents belonged to no party although they were rather left of centre. I did not join the Labour Party until after I came to Putney. One of the reasons was that it was the first place in which I seemed settled and it had a Labour MP. I'd always lived in Tory areas before so that was very nice. I also decided that it was no use staying outside the party because there were things about it I did not like and that people like me ought to join because if you don't like what the party is doing you can't complain if you're on the outside. I rang up the Party Headquarters one day in the early seventies and was invited to attend the Annual General Meeting. I went along and joined.

I was drawn into activity from the beginning. Ward meetings were sometimes interesting and well attended but sometimes not, even when we had a visiting speaker. Very soon I was on the General Management Committee but it took me some time, even a few months, before I found out who people were and what was going on. At the beginning everyone seemed to know exactly what was happening except me. You have to persist a little bit to find out what it's all about but there was enough which struck a chord with me to make it worthwhile to get to know about it and to know the members.

Some time later there was an aldermanic vacancy on the Council, one of the last before Aldermen were abolished, and I was asked to take it and accepted. I came on in the middle of the Council and once again had to spend time finding my way about. My term of office finished in 1978 and I stood for election as a Councillor after that but was defeated. While I was on the Council I served on the Housing Committee, Housing Development, Policy Review Sub-committee and Social Services.

We lost control of the Council partly because of the national swing against Labour and partly because, as we were in power locally, all the

127

complaints were laid at our door. There was also in some parts of the Borough a change against Labour in the political complexion. I'm not sorry to be out of the Council in a way because all those who are still there tell me how depressing it is to be in opposition and to see all the things we worked for being dismantled.

Being active in the Labour Party soon becomes part of one's life and one reason why I joined was a desire to be involved in forming policies. Being on the GMC also keeps you in touch with the other members of the party from different wards or branches as we now say. I think the Putney Party has had some influence on national policy; it's very hard to know but as we are always debating and sending off resolutions and letting people know what we are thinking it surely must have some effect. It *must* matter. There's a lot of disillusion with politics both inside and outside the party and this worries me because I think the party ought to be forming its policies both nationally and locally. We've got to come back knowing what we want to do and there's not enough being done on this.

I've made a lot of friends in the Putney Party and in London that's important especially for someone who lives alone like me. Belonging to the party bases you in the area of London where you live. In a small town there's not the same problem but in London belonging and being active in the local party makes you a part of the local community.

There's quite a big turnover in Putney and in the short time I've been here the people who make up the ward and GMC have changed quite a bit; there are only a few long-term old-timers. Now that the welfare state is being dismantled we shall have to re-state the case outside the party; it can no longer be taken for granted; education too, when we were in office we never really came to grips with the independent schools, they should have been taken into the state system, if that had happened it would have been difficult for the Tories to turn the clock back. Then take the state of the health serivce; if only we had been more resolute about private beds. As for health service dentistry it seems to be disappearing.

What else do you do in the party?

I'm our Ward Membership Officer and a delegate to the Local Government Committee and I'm now Treasurer of that Committee. I'm also on the Party Executive Committee. The Local Government Committee, among other things, is responsible for municipal election policy. I'm very worried now by the Tory policy of selling houses because the people in need are never going to be able to buy in an area like this. This is not something we can put right when we get back because there's no more land — it's gone for good. I don't see how we are ever going to be able to build up the housing stock again. I'm also worried about unemployment and people having no work to go to when they leave school. So what with worries and jobs I've enough to keep me occupied.

HUGH STEPHENSON

41. Editor of The Times Business News.
Journalist and broadcaster. Married to
another journalist. Also a member of the Labour
Party. They have three children.

I first joined the Labour Party at university, I think out of curiosity to begin with. I came from an unpolitical but Conservative family and I went to America and then into the civil service and I didn't really become active in the party until we came to Putney in 1966. However I then went to Germany for two years and so I didn't really get going until 1968. I've been fairly active since then.

The morale of the party was very low at that time, ward meetings were poorly attended and it wasn't really a good time to get active in the party. I remember the Thamesfield Ward rejecting a membership drive on the grounds that it was useless to expect people to join at that time; it was a depressing period but the Thamesfield Ward was very friendly. Things improved in the run up to the 1970 general election which you and we were all surprised and delighted to win in Putney although we lost office nationally. Nevertheless, in Putney morale continued to improve; we won control of the Borough Council and that gave all of us a focus; that was in May 1971. However bad our fortunes have been since we have never been anywhere near as low as we were in 1968 when the support of the party seemed to be draining away. It's never been like that since and it's not like that now.

In 1971, rather by accident, I became a member of the Council. Thamesfield was held by the Tories and selected its candidates late. By the time Thamesfield was allowed to select its three there was no one left on the panel whom the Thamesfield Ward wanted. A month later a second selection conference was held and three people were selected, none of whom had been on the original panel. They were Elizabeth Rackham, Brian Sedgemoor and myself and we were rather drafted. We were surprised to become Councillors as Thamesfield was not thought of as a likely Labour win. I did two terms on the Council, seven years altogether and I was even more surprised to be re-elected on the second occasion. It was an extremely interesting seven years in which I learned a great deal about local government. One of the most striking things was the way in which, while governments of both parties talk a lot about local autonomy and decentralising decisions, you

130

simply saw, in those seven years, the decision-making process being centralised and taken away from local government by governments of both persuasions. The two things which brought this about more than others were the Conservative Housing Finance Act and Labour's decisions on comprehensive education.

The Conservative Act sought to impose on every local authority in the country exactly what they had to do about rent increases. A local authority is elected to be above most other things, a housing authority; if you mean what you say about autonomy you should allow local authorities to handle their own housing but the Housing Finance Act and legal action against the Clay Cross Councillors forced every local authority in the country to toe the line.

Later on, and for perfectly good motives (I was not opposed to the policy itself) the incoming Labour Government tried to force every authority in the country to introduce comprehensive education. Not being an education authority we were not affected in Wandsworth but these two measures are examples of the fact that governments in this country don't mean what they say about local autonomy and when it comes to it, central government policy is imposed. The tendency is for more and more centralisation. It comes about for another reason; when I first joined the Council in 1971, in rough terms two-thirds of its revenue came from the rates and one-third from central government; seven years later it was almost exactly the other way round — one-third from the rates and two-thirds from the government's rate support grant. When that happened and the majority of local government expenditure began to be found by the national government then the person paying the piper would inevitably assert his right to call the tune. Power in local authorities has been drawn away and the mechanics of it is the issue of circulars from central government telling local authorities what to do and what not to do. Quite often Councillors don't see these circulars which go from civil servants to senior local government officials and members subsequently discover that they and all other authorities up and down the country are doing the same thing.

I think the tendency to centralisation will remain strong because our people have a highly developed sense of equity; people think it unfair if people in two neighbouring areas get different services or different levels of service; if these become blatant the pressure to equalise them will always be there. The only way in which you can make a reality of devolution — Scotland, regional government, anything — is if the body you create has taxing powers so that it is actually responsible to its electorate for what it spends and has to raise a significant part of the money from them.

I've had no difficulty in my work arising from my political convictions apart from the purely mechanical fact that I tend to work rather late and gained a reputation among my colleagues on the Council of being late for evening meetings. This was one reason why I never attempted to become a chairman of a committee. Being a Councillor puts an extraordinary strain on family life because night after night you are not at home and although one's wife and children are very understanding it is not an ideal version of what family life should be about. It unquestionably puts a strain on peoples' lives and during my seven years on the Council I saw several perfectly good marriages break up. My wife shares my political views; she is a member of the Labour Party and although we don't have identical views on everything, we broadly agree.

I was on the Finance Committee of the Council throughout my period of office on the Council and on other committees from time to time. Council work is not very efficiently conducted and one got frustrated from time to time by the amount of time one had to sit there while not very efficient papers were presented not very efficiently in crowded rooms late at night, but apart from that I enjoyed the work. When we gained control of the Council in 1971 there was a clean sweep and most of us were new to Council work, even some of the Committee Chairmen and we took a long time to discover how the system actually worked; to begin to use it instead of allowing it to use us; we therefore became more than usually dominated by the officers and particularly by the Town Clerk. It was not until later that the Labour Group as a whole, and some of the Committee Chairmen individually, began to know how to get things done. I think we did ourselves political damage in things like our housing policy where we failed to co-ordinate between what we knew we wanted done and what was actually happening on the ground. For example, we adopted a policy of buying up houses when the housing boom collapsed and for a time the Council was the only major house buyer in the area. The policy was extremely sensible but because we did not control the machine those houses remained empty and boarded up for scandalously long periods. The Tories made a considerable political meal of this and it did us a lot of damage.

After I'd been a Councillor for seven years I felt that that was long enough to be out for as many nights as Council work entails but apart from that it became apparent that we were not going to hold Thamesfield Ward and as I think Councillors should live in the wards they represent (they make better Councillors if they do because it's much easier to understand what people are worked up about if you live in the area), I decided not to stand. But I would certainly do it all over again.

Ian McGarry was elected Leader of the Council in 1971; I thought then and think now that he was and is one of the most able politicians I have met. He resigned as the result of the fracas over the Conservative Housing Finance Act which split the Labour Group from top to bottom and the group was pretty leaderless for a while. Later we had John Tilley until he became an MP. He is very able. But in seven years we had five leadership changes and that didn't help. Much of the early part was taken up with petty fratricidal strife because the Group had split so completely and so bitterly over housing finance and people became unfair in their judgement of each other. This dominated personal relationships for a time but even so there were on the Council many people of real ability as well as some who had succeeded to chairmanships as the result of long service and good conduct.

It is also the case that both Ward and General Management Committee meetings have become more and more interesting in recent years. Today they are well attended and I am constantly pleased and surprised by the level of interest attained by invited speakers and the level of the following discussion. I have been a member of the General Management Committee throughout the period.

I suppose the hard core of members is quite small; one tends to see the same faces at meetings and jumble sales and fetes; but it increases at election times and you get 30 or 40 or even 50 people turning up for canvassing on the estates and elsewhere. Still, I suppose the majority of members are just subscription payers but I've been struck that at times when the party is not doing very well there have still been a steady trickle of new members joining the party; very encouraging.

Do you think it strikes your colleagues or your readers as a little odd that the Editor of The Times Business News should be a member of the Labour Party?

Clearly journalists in senior positions who are also members of the Labour Party are in a minority. It's widely known now that I am and I've largely forgotten the element of surprise that was there in the first place but I think bankers and others *are* surprised to learn that you're a card-carrying member of the party. I've never hidden it and it does not embarrass me at all. What I have tried to do, obviously, is so to conduct my journalism so that no one could ever say 'He's written that from a narrow party political point of view.' No one ever has.

What appeals to you about being a member of the Labour Party?

I think that the democratic political process is important and if you think that then you'd better get up and do something about it. As a rank and file member of the Putney Party I don't think I have any feeling of having influenced the course of events but a local Councillor certainly has some influence. In that area one has a strong feeling of having influenced things, planning matters and otherwise. For a party which in its rhetoric and in its heart believes in democracy, there are some pretty undemocratic corners in it and the same applies to large chunks of the trade union movement. Therefore, if you are going to move in the direction of more democratic control, there are areas of our machinery which require examination. Even in London there are constituency Labour parties which are akin to rotten boroughs, which are run by small cliques and I cannot believe this is healthy for the party. None of that seems to me to apply to the Putney Labour Party which is conspicuously open and democratic; there is obviously a left and a centre and a right to it but it has never struck me as a party which has fallen into the hands of one clique.

I am wholly in favour of more democratic influence on governments in office and on the parliamentary party in opposition but for that to happen the party as a whole needs to look at the reforms required to make it more democratic itself.

What do you dislike about being a member of the party?

I am not terribly enthusiastic about fetes which are called in our family fetes worse than death; there do seem to be a lot of them and I understand their function as a social and fund-raising thing but I sometimes feel they have little to do with political activity and are not terribly efficient as a means of raising funds.

You've never been a parliamentary candidate have you?

No. I've thought about it a great deal and a few years ago I would have been very keen if the opportunity had arisen but at the age of 41 I am not so sure. I think I may now never become a parliamentary candidate and I don't think I shall try to return to the Council, at least not for many years, not until the children are fully grown up.

JUDITH CHEGWIDDEN

*33. Single. Born in Truro, Cornwall. Came to
Wandsworth while studying at London University.
Now a partner in a firm of industrial consultants
and a Labour Councillor.*

My membership of the Labour Party is a complete breakaway from
family background. My father was a non-political schoolmaster and my
mother a convinced Tory. I came up to London in 1964 and was
excited at the idea of a new Labour Government. I joined in student
politics but it wasn't until I got a job and moved to Putney that I
actually joined the party. That was in 1971 and within two months I
was Secretary of the Putney Branch and on the General Management
Committee. I have been an active member ever since. The Labour Party
had lost the 1970 general election and I felt guilty about not having
done anything to help but I did not join with the idea of becoming so
involved as it has turned out. Putney Branch was in chaos and I was
simply plunged into it. My mother and I never discuss politics. We get
on well otherwise so we simply leave it alone.

Putney Ward was full of articulate and active people and I found the
meetings enjoyable. I was interested and acquired more knowledge as I
went along. There were stimulating debates, more so then than lately.

I went on a selection panel and eventually became a Labour
Councillor in 1974 for the Springfield Ward and I've been on the
Council ever since. When Labour was in power I was Chairman of the
Housing Development Sub-committee and Vice-chairman of the
Housing Committee. Since we have been out of office it has been
heart-breaking watching the Tories arrogantly smashing up our
Housing and Social Service policies.

I like where I work. It's a small company and I've since become a
partner. Everyone is relaxed about me being on the Council and taking
time off for that. We work hard but we're not in a rat race. We're
basically industrial marketing consultants but we are fairly specialised
and mainly concerned with minerals and metals. We establish industrial
markets for particular products.

You're not married or anything?

No. I'm buying my own house here in Putney as you know. You get
used to living alone and probably get more difficult to live with all the

time. I'm not very ambitious I think. I like what I'm doing and want to go on doing it. Once you've made a commitment to Council work it becomes part of your life. Other things get pushed on one side and you tend to gravitate towards the things and the people — you become involved and it would be a big wrench to change. I try to keep some other interests but my work, the Council, and the party become the main things. I get great satisfaction out of dealing with local issues or nowadays fighting the Tories and trying to stop them from doing so much damage.

I think the party is dispirited at the moment after losing the Council, the Greater London Council and then the general election. We need some victories to buck us up. We are tending to agree with each other, to avoid contentious issues and meetings are getting boring. All this concentration on structure and democracy in the party is squeezing out discussion on issues. We must be careful not to antagonise the trade unions or the democracy argument will be lost. It's time to look at our economic policies again, incomes policy or free collective bargaining and so on. At present we take on the easy things and put down resolutions on which most of us will agree. A good win in a Council by-election would do us a lot of good and send our morale up. As for the frustrations of party work, well, they are part of the game and it never occurs to me to think that I'll give up the Labour Party because of them. I think I keep on hoping. (Laughs.) There's no real alternative, is there? I think I'm lucky being on the Council. It keeps me occupied. I could always get out if I wanted to but I've never wanted to. Party work gives you a sense of obligation, not only to the party but to the people you're working with and there's nothing wrong with having a sense of obligation. It's not a bad idea having to do something not very exciting in itself, like delivering leaflets, because you believe in what you're doing it for. It's especially good for someone like me because there are very few other things in my life I *do* have a sense of obligation about. My mother is far from being dependent upon me and I have no other close relatives. We find it difficult to talk about the party in these terms but sometimes it's good to ask yourself why you are in the party; not that there's any problem of identity when you're on the Council and have to watch what the Tories are doing. It's easier to know what you're against than what you're for. When you're in power you feel the frustrations of not being able to do all you want to do.

When we were in charge of the Wandsworth Borough Council we had no compunction whatsoever in publicly disagreeing with our Labour Government when they wouldn't allow us to do all we wanted to do. The Tories are very different; subservient and obedient to authority. They maintain a united front with their government and Central Office but I think our open disagreements are best in spite of what the press does to us as a result. People like to see local people standing up for local benefits. It was not until a great deal of pressure from us and others that the Labour Government put a ban on the sale of Council housing property. I think we are more honest in local government than the Tories. We put up the rates when they needed to be put up instead of fudging the accounts until after the election and we paid for that honesty; we got thrown out. Perhaps we were too honest but it is not right to try to hide from the electorate that the Labour Party is likely to be a high rate party. But, of course, you can go too far with it and there were people in the Putney end of the Borough who found our rate increase a real burden. But I don't think we lost office only because of that; it was partly due to the unpopularity of the Labour Government at that time.

The party should be looking into such things as the redistribution of wealth and not only by means of taxation. There's a lot to be done but I think my own contribution will remain chiefly local. I like the way local politics work; I like the committee system; I like the way all elected Councillors share in the responsibility of running the Council. Cabinet government no longer seems to work very well, if it ever did, so perhaps national government has something to learn from local government in involving all members of the ruling party in the processes of government. For myself I hope I shall be allowed to play some part in clearing up the Tory mess when we return to power in Wandsworth in 1982.

ROGER GOULBORN

Age 32. Full-time trade union officer. Married
with two young children.

We came to live in Putney in 1972. I was already married and working
with the union at that time as a Research Officer. I had steered clear of
political organisations in college and did not join the Labour Party as
an individual member until we came to Putney. I wanted to be an
active member, not one in name only and it was not difficult for me
to get on to the General Management Committee as a trade union
delegate. My branch was affiliated to the Putney Labour Party and
like many trade unions we did not take up the full delegation to which
our contribution entitled us. This enabled me to plunge straight away
into active party work.

Putney had a reputation as a leftish party and I found the party here
active and politically aware. There is no background of political activity
in my family but while I was at university studying industrial relations
and doing a lot of reading I formed socialist convictions, initially from
purely academic sources. The ideas of the left seemed to me to make
the most sense and to form a coherent basis for political belief. If you
are interested in politics you need some area where you can debate and
listen to opinions; if politics are not dynamic they're dead and
membership of the party and participation in meetings provides the
opportunity for ideas to be tested and argued.

The party has become bureaucratic and some improvements should
be made in its democratic structure. The average party member has
little influence over national policies but he can make his voice heard
on local matters for some of the local Councillors are themselves likely
to be on the GMC. There they can be encouraged or criticised but
some leading Members of Parliament seem to take pride in being
beyond control or even influence. MPs must be made more accountable,
while that is not the case there is no devolution of power down the rank
and file.

Anyone who believes in what the Labour Party stands for; in a
socialist society, has an obligation to be a member of the party. My job
prevents me from being as active as I should like to be.

As you know my trade union allowed me to spend some of my time
helping Putney at the last three general elections. I felt we were likely
to lose in 1979; in retrospect it was the collapse of the Liberal vote

that sank us. At election time there is a different approach. The events cause you to get very mechanistic and put questions of political philosophy into cold storage.

Many active trade unionists are also active members of their local Labour parties, the conflict is not between the constituencies and the trade unions but inside the trade union movement and the Labour Party; in both cases it is a conflict between leadership and rank and file but, of course, that is a simplification, it is more complex than that. Nearly all rank and file constituency members are also trade unionists. The forces against change are very strong, so the initiative which came from the unions for an examination of Labour Party structure is one which should be welcomed. The party cannot go on as at present organised for it is in decline rather than in growth; the contributions are too low, we are disastrously short of full-time Agents; there is something to be said for state support for political parties but I am not in favour of anything which would loosen the relationships between the party and the trade unions.

As for incomes policies, I am not in favour of a policy which seeks to hold down wages while all other indices are climbing; that is a device to make working people pay for the inadequacy of the present economic system. On the other hand no one can say he would *never* be in favour of an incomes policy and still call himself a socialist; in a fully planned economy, incomes must be a part of the plan. I have a fairly pessimistic view about the future of the British economy but Labour must be ready to fight for the next general election on a socialist alternative to the present chaos.

I was born in the United States and brought up in Switzerland but I went to Cheltenham Ladies College and to Hull and Oxford universities where I joined the Labour Party. My parents were socialists. At a mock election at school I was the only Labour Party supporter!

While I was at Oxford, at Ruskin College, I became a candidate for the local Council and eventually a Councillor. I fought Henley in the 1970 parliamentary election, a safe Tory seat, of course, and Reading, which we thought we might win, in the two 1974 elections. We lost by 468 on the second occasion. Then my parents, who had lived in Putney before going abroad, sold me their house here where my husband and I now live. I joined the Putney Labour Party, that was in 1976, and have been on the General Management Committee as well. I have experience of several Labour parties now and Putney is the least bitchy of the lot. I'm not in the middle of the Putney Labour Party but with Putney you never feel that people are gunning for someone. There's no sense of using political differences to emphasise personal differences, none of 'that left-wing cow' or 'that right-wing bastard', you don't get this in Putney and it's pretty rare in my experience not to get it.

I fought Derbyshire in the 1979 European elections and we ought to have won it but the Labour vote simply refused to turn out in any strength. I was not chosen for the general election of 1979 and in my experience it is a disadvantage to be a woman. One has no sense of that in Putney, indeed I fought the last Council election here, the one we lost, of course! Putney is a left-wing party but tolerantly so. It is also almost obsessively hard-working demanding more of its members and especially GMC members than any other party in my experience. Putney Labour Party sweats; there are deliveries or something almost every Sunday, it goes on and on and on. If you are a member of the Putney GMC, you are aware of the fact almost all the time. To some extent the party determines your life, it is very present and powerful. There's a strong sense of obligation.

In my search for a parliamentary seat I've been badly hurt. It's very difficult for a woman to get selected for a safe seat. I've been told flat out, 'I hope you get selected somewhere but we're not interested in women here.'

MIKE GAPES

27. MA Econ. (Cambs) Labour Party's
National Student Organiser.

Putney's Labour Party is very friendly. I came to live here by chance three years ago and I was really impressed by the way I was made to feel welcome. Members of the Putney Party seem to be active not only in the party but in other areas as well. One thing we seem to lack is active manual workers; we ought to involve more people in our active work and especially from our traditional supporters. Nevertheless Putney is probably amongst the most active Labour parties in the country.

I was always very interested in politics even when I was at school. From the age of twelve or thirteen I was involved in talking and debating political issues and joined the Labour Party at 16 as soon as I was eligible. My father was a trade union Branch Secretary but not an individual Labour Party member until I persuaded him to join quite recently. I got my father, my mother and my brother to join on the same day — it was in 1974 and in that election my grandmother voted for the first time.

I've been on the General Management Committee here for two years; I'm Political Education Officer and I enjoy the work; I'm on the Executive Committee and now I'm Chairman of the Thamesfield Branch having previously been Membership Officer, so I'm pretty active. I really enjoy the Thamesfield meetings, we have a good lively branch and we seldom get less than 20 people to our meetings. There is no conflict between my full-time job with the Labour Party and my constituency work because I am a specialist but if I worked, say, in the Regional Office there might be problems. My only trouble is shortage of time!

I have a lot to do with youth and I find that many young people don't join the Young Socialists but prefer to be ordinary party members and be active in the party rather than join the YS. The potential for youth involvement in the party is very great but I don't think we've tapped that potential properly either in Putney or nationally. There are a variety of reasons for that, one is the way in which we appeal to young people trying to apply traditional methods to a generation brought up in the television age. We could learn from the success of the Anti-Nazi League and the big anti-racist carnivals.

141

These have included Labour Party members but are not organised by the party. We can learn a lesson from this on questions of youth unemployment, the rights of young people, democracy in education, school students' unions; these are the issues many young people are concerned about.

Another problem is that constitutionally the Young Socialists run from 15 to 25 years old. I'm not sure that that's right. I think it might be better to follow the example of other countries where the youth organisations start much younger. We ought to think of the nine-year-olds and upwards and try to involve them in youth activities. I've done a fair bit of international travelling and, for example in Sweden and Germany, they have very strong organisations for young people at those earlier ages. Here, we have thought that the Co-operative Woodcraft Folk would cover that role but they don't really — their scope and range is limited. They do a very useful job but the Labour Party itself has taken no initiative in that area.

I don't agree that the Labour Party is in decline. At present, parties have to affiliate on 1,000 members and may do so. When they have less than 1,000 no one would know. The percentage who are active is a small one but this has always been the case. The question we really ought to ask is what percentage play an active role within the party. It would be easy to have a large paper membership, based on, for example, fund-raising tote schemes, which was not involved. My view is that the number of active people in the Labour Party today is probably as high as it was in previous years. The interesting question is whether those activists feel that they are listened to enough and have as large a role within the party as they should. This is a very topical question and it lies behind the constitutional debate in the party. I believe that there should be a significant shift towards greater involvement of active party members and away from traditional Burkeian concepts of government. The Conservative model of parliamentary democracy; the power of the Prime Minister and the Executive, has been transposed, imported, into the Labour movement and it has been kept there, sometimes by negligence, sometimes by design. This has had consequences within the structure of the party. I think the proposals for automatic re-selection of MPs are quite sensible, but in themselves they won't radically change the nature of the party in Parliament. I can't see the arguments against the election of the Leader by an electoral college or by Conference. Of all the social democratic parties I know the only one which has the same system as Britain is New Zealand; in Scandinavia, in Germany, in Australia, in all the others throughout the world, the socialist movement has always found a means to involve active party members, the constituencies, the trade unions. I don't see why the Conservative tradition of the dominance of the MP with a role representing and mediating interests rather than as a spokesman and delegate for the Labour movement, I don't see why that tradition should be allowed to override the internal democracy of the Labour Party.

There are obviously people in the party who don't want change, some of them use arguments which emanate from the concept of parliamentary authority and the role of the Prime Minister as dispenser of patronage; others use more sophisticated arguments but ultimately it's a question of who are the activists within the party, who determine the policy of the party and how is that policy to be translated into political action by a Labour Government. I think that if the Party Conference had a larger say and the National Executive had a larger say in the actions of a Labour Government you would find that instead of the present broad general resolutions 'We're all against sin' you would get much more detailed discussions and more sophisticated discussions on particular issues.

There *is* a problem at the moment. Let's say your individual activist puts a resolution to a branch and it is passed; it goes to the General Committee and is carried there too; let's suppose it goes to Annual Conference and is passed there too; let's even suppose it gets carried by a two-thirds majority on a card vote so it should go in the programme. If it's included in the programme it just conceivably might under the old system, let us suppose, go through the next stage of being selected by the NEC and the Cabinet for inclusion in the election manifesto. Even then there is still no guarantee that a Labour Government will carry it out. They can argue lack of a majority, lack of legislative time, pressures from the International Monetary Fund; opposition from the CBI or other special interests; hostility or prevarication from the civil service; weakness of the Minister or any other reason for it not to happen. That's a very long and difficult process so it's not surprising that Conference resolutions are sometimes a bit simplistic, anything more detailed gets lost in the process.

The Labour Party in Putney is in the mainstream of the left. The left in the party is a very broad concept, the spectrum of different groups and newspapers is quite massive but Putney has a large number of activists who are committed to the policies of the Party Conference and to the National Executive Committee's attempts to secure greater democracy in the party. We also have some people who disagree with that; some who might think of themselves as further left and others who would more support the Leader of the Opposition and the parliamentary leadership generally. This is today repeated throughout the country nationally; this is a big change from what I understand used to be the case; there has been a move against deferential behaviour towards the leadership; a realisation that this does not bring socialism, that you have to be a bit aggressive and a bit critical, sometimes even publicly, in order to bring about changes that most people want today. On the other hand the leadership is subject to all kinds of countervailing pressures so let us hope that they would welcome the pressure we exert in the other direction.

When I moved to Putney in 1976 I came to a ward which had Labour Councillors who made up part of a Labour majority on the Council. We had a Labour GLC Representative in Marie and a Labour MP in yourself. I don't know if it's anything to do with me but we've now lost all of them! We have to return to more campaigning work locally as well as nationally in opposition to the Tory cuts — the callous face of local Thatcherism. The consequences of the extremely reactionary Tory Council we have here in Wandsworth will mean that the electorate will turn to the Labour Party again to clear up the disastrous mess that the Tories will leave us to clear up in the eighties. Similarly I think we shall recover control of the Greater London Council. In Putney we must gain support from people who have moved into the constituency recently. We have to be outward-going and put across our ideas in ways people understand. We mustn't preach to people or talk down to them. We must tell them the facts, put them on the line, say what we believe in; we must never try to pretend to believe something we do not, in order to get votes. The future of the country could well be decided by ten or fifteen constituencies such as Putney in the south of England. So we have to put a lot of effort into it, not only in terms of policies but in perfecting our organisation.

Putney's a pleasant place to live in. I've put some roots down and I'm quite happy here. I know I'm going to be involved in politics in one form or another for the rest of my life, it's in my blood now. I don't think I'm going to stay in my current job much longer — there's an age problem in student politics and although I enjoy the job I think I shall have to make a move soon. I want to remain active in a political job in the movement either in the civil service of the party as a political organiser or elsewhere in a position which would allow me to remain an active member.

In my life so far my involvement in the Labour Party has been one of the most important things in it. Another very important influence was the year I spent teaching in Voluntary Service Overseas in Swaziland. The effect of this on me was profound for I was next door to South Africa and Swaziland was economically dominated by the country of apartheid. You can read about things and you can understand the situation but you can't get the feel of what it's like unless you stay in the country. Since then when I've been involved in campaigning against apartheid, for disinvestment in South Africa, against Rugby tours and so on, I've been able to say to people, I *do* know what the situation is like because I've been there, I've seen it, I've got friends there, I've taught there. My opposition to racism in all its forms is much stronger and deeper and it's not just an abstract response, because of that year in Africa. I've recently been back on holiday to see people I used to teach who are now doing a variety of jobs; it's been very good to be able to talk to people and to get to know what they think of the latest developments.

*44. Born in South Africa. Brought up
and went to university there. Active in
the student movement. Had some difficulty in
getting out of South Africa.*

In 1960 I finally decided to leave South Africa and settle in this
country. After belonging to movements such as CND I suddenly
realised that I needed a political base. At the time I was a married
student, living in Putney and in about 1963 I decided to join the Labour
Party here, went up to 168 Upper Richmond Road, joined and became
involved. About then I moved to West Hill and Len Holmes came
round to see me. He invited me to a ward meeting and straight away I
was given a collecting book and that's how it began.

I didn't come into the Labour Party because of the class struggle or
as the result of reading Marx. At that time I was a typical, woolly, airy,
liberal, enlightened on social things, worried about the aftermath of
Suez, about racism and rents, all that. Soon I was on the General
Management Committee.

I started work by teaching but decided that was not for me, studied
architecture and eventually became an architect. I now work for
Southwark Council as leader of a group of architects redeveloping the
Surrey Docks part of Southwark. It's really a new town inside London
and I think one of the best jobs an architect could have.

West Hill was a very active ward at the time I joined but when I got
on to the GMC I realised that this was the *politically* active area. They
gave me a real fright. I didn't know very much about socialism, nor
did I know any active trade unionists. I'm still slightly middle-class
and then it was astonishing to me to find that there were young
working-class people and older people who were articulate and could
express themselves and say things I was after but never quite understood.
It was like a spark lighting up and for four or five years it was a
marvellous educative time for me — very exciting.

I was elected to the Council in 1971. I'd become involved in the
Fairfield Ward with Peter and Maria Marshall who were trying to get
work done on the old East Hill Estate. They had the idea of reducing
the density on the estate by pulling part of it down and rehabilitating
the rest. Because I was an architect they asked me to help them in
preparing plans and so on. We produced a report which we gave to the

Council but because the Tories were in control at the time they refused to look at it. The matter became an election issue in the Borough elections, I was invited to accept nomination and was duly elected in that fairly safe Labour ward.

There was a tremendous changeover from Tory to Labour at that election and most of the new members of the Council had little experience. Ian McGarry became Leader, I became Chairman of the Highways Committee and went on to the Planning Committee and the Building Works Committee. It was especially enjoyable for me, as an architect, to be on the Planning Committee. Then we had the big upset caused by the Tory Housing Finance Act. The Council was controlled by a progressive group but the Tory Government put the screws on and this shifted the balance on the Council. It was agreed that the rents should be raised as demanded by the Tories, or as laid down by the law. Leading members of the Council were very unhappy at this and a number of us resigned our positions including Ian McGarry and myself. For best part of a year there was a total balls-up. We were at each others throats. We of the 'left' were, perhaps, a little insensitive in our criticisms but we were determined to get back into office and we did in less than a year. We had to compromise by raising the rents to some extent and we had a lot of criticism for that.

I then became Chairman of the Policy and Resources Committee and later Deputy Leader of the Council. Fairfield was taken away from Putney by the Boundary Commission and as I wanted to remain a Putney Councillor I put up in Roehampton and was chosen. It always astonishes me that working-class wards choose obviously middle-class people like me to represent them.

Then my marriage broke up. I got divorced and was living in North Battersea and, representing a Putney ward, it became very difficult for me to do the job properly. I decided I had to stop. It was a personal decision, nothing to do with politics. First I stepped down as Deputy Leader and as Committee Chairman and became an ordinary Councillor but I did not stand again at the next Borough elections. That was in 1978. Now I'm back in the Putney constituency and I hope to re-marry soon. My main public work at the moment is that I'm Chairman of the Board of Governors of Southfields School.

During my years as a member of the Putney General Management Committee I was selected as delegate to Annual Conference twice. On the first occasion Putney put forward a motion on public schools, it went into the Composite Resolution which I seconded but it was accepted by the National Executive with a reservation about our piece and, of course, the public schools have never been abolished. I had made

147

a study of the subject as a member of a committee headed by Caroline Benn and it was a very exciting time for me — both enjoyable and politically exciting.

The second time I was there our resolution was composited with motions put forward by some of the large trade unions and we never got a nose in.

There was another interesting thing. Once I was put on a disciplinary committee concerning some misdemeanour by one of our Councillors. Nothing came of it. The Putney Party has always been very tolerant in my experience I'm glad to say.

DOROTHY TARRY

*Married, tall, blonde; looks too young
to have three teenaged children.
Recently graduated as a BSc (Econ.) –
now working as a research assistant and
reading for a PhD. Husband, David,
himself a PhD is a veterinary entomologist
employed by the civil service and an
amateur musician in the local
symphony orchestra.*

We came to Putney from Richmond in 1970. We were already Labour
voters, but had not yet joined the Labour Party at this time, although
we worked alongside Labour members in various pressure groups in
Richmond, such as CND, the Richmond Council for Peace in
Vietnam, and a group formed to pressurise the local Council into
introducing comprehensive schooling in the area. During the period of
the Wilson Governments from 1964 to 1970, we had not felt impelled
to join the Labour Party, as we were out of sympathy with many of
the government policies, and particularly with government foreign
policy. However, when we came to Putney, just before the 1970
general election, we felt convinced that the Conservatives would win
the election, and in these circumstances we decided we should make a
firm commitment to the Labour Party, and try to work within it. There
was no tradition of party membership, nor indeed of Labour voting,
in my family, and I came to the party interested in abstract ideals of
social justice and the need to oppose oppression wherever it might be
found, rather than in the necessary mechanics of keeping a political
party viable, active and effective. However, when we joined the Putney
Labour Party, we became immediately involved in the election
campaign, and we have been active members ever since, although my
husband's commitment to the local symphony orchestra has meant
that he has not been able to become quite so deeply involved in the
day-to-day running of the Labour Party as I have myself.

When David and I were married, we went to live in Northern
Nigeria, where he was already employed by the Nigerian Government
as an entomologist working on a tsetse fly eradication scheme. We
lived for over a year in a grass hut in the heart of the Ningi Bush, until
I became pregnant and had to leave for home. Our time in the Bush

149

was a time of unusual hardship, but also of unusual interest, and I think this period in our lives confirmed my interest in international political issues, and especially in the problems facing the countries of the Third World.

On our return from Nigeria, David had to find employment in what is a very restricted field, but finally he was able to find a job as a veterinary entomologist with the civil service.

On the day we joined the Labour Party, we were immediately sent out with a party of canvassers to Southfields. We coped with this by observing and imitating other canvassers in the group, and afterwards we all went for a drink. We quickly established common interests and became friends. In this way, we were soon deeply involved in party activities. I started to attend ward meetings regularly (later becoming Ward Secretary) and I soon had a place on the General Management Committee. Unfortunately, these meetings clashed with David's orchestra rehearsal nights, so he was unable to attend. Once I was a member of the General Management Committee, I began to feel closer to the centre of things. For instance, I could now follow through a resolution passed by my branch, and know something of its final fate. I could also participate in the general decision making process of the party.

I have never seriously considered becoming a member of the Council, because my family, my work, my study and my ordinary Labour Party work fully occupy my time. I have served as Local Government Committee observer on the Labour Group of the Council, and I am well aware of the extent of the commitment required of a Councillor if he is to be effective.

What I like about being an active party member is that it allows me to meet with like-minded people. I like to be with them, whether we agree or disagree, or just joke about things together. I am not a passive person, so it is natural for me to be involved in matters beyond my own personal concerns, anyway. I would rather beat my head against a brick wall than stand by and do nothing. I think for many of us who are political activists, it is less painful to seek to achieve some end, even if it looks impossible, than to allow events to happen without making any effort to affect their course. We know that many of the resolutions we fight to get through may well end up in someone's waste-paper basket, but we cannot allow that consideration to deter us from passing the resolutions in the first place.

This brings me to a consideration of the less enjoyable aspects of being a Labour Party activist: there is often a feeling of frustration and impotence, a sense that those at the top of the party regard the grass roots activists as no more than components of a vote-gathering machine, who have no business concerning themselves with the formulation of party policy. The mundane business of attending committees, raising funds and 'vote-gathering' can be quite tedious, and activists need recognition that they undertake these tasks in order that certain objectives may be pursued, and that certain ideals will not be sacrificed. I am a realist rather than a Utopian, but I am a firm believer in the welfare state, and I expect to see the National Health Service, employment, education, housing and social services preserved by any Labour Government; that is why I am a Labour Party worker.

Looking back, there was something pleasurable in being in opposition under the Heath Government; we could attack them instead of our own leadership, and to some extent we could safeguard local services, because we still had control of the Council. The Wilson—Callaghan period which followed was a sad one in many ways; we saw the welfare state being eroded, and this is particularly dispiriting for the Labour Party. Of course I recognise that this was partly because the Labour Party was in a minority in Parliament, and partly the result of international crises and the pressure of the IMF, but some of us felt that political will had gone out of the party leadership. High office sometimes seems to sap radicalism, and this affects the party badly, because we want our ideals kept alive. We find ourselves wondering which of our potential leaders would retain his or her will and energy for socialism should he or she become Prime Minister.

I think the rank and file ought to have more influence. I would not like the Labour Party to decline into a simple vote-getting machine so I would like the parliamentary party and the government when we have one to be more responsive to local pressures but I should also like us to have a much larger membership. We ought to be much more of a mass party than we are instead of one with a declining membership.

Have you ever thought of primary elections?

I think I've toyed with most ideas by now. But I'm not sure how primaries would fit into the British system. In the American system, parties really only exist at election times, and the primaries have an obvious place. It is often thought that introducing primaries into the British system would heighten party democracy. But, paradoxically, it could separate the rank and file of the party even further from the decision-making process. Their sole function might finally be to drum up support for some candidate or other. Moreover, the system would be

151

open to misuse and even corruption. Inducements of a more or less tangible nature might be offered to those who would join the party to support a certain candidate. This would entirely change our notions of party membership. Perhaps we should consider finding some means of including party members who attend branch meetings regularly, but are not on the GMC, in the selection process. Their services certainly deserve some recognition. But I don't know how party regulations allowing their involvement could be formulated.

Which aspects of party work displease you most?

Certainly not the political arguments. They can be very interesting. But, of course, there are many intensely boring activities connected with party work. No one can pretend that addressing 800 envelopes or folding the same number of leaflets, is a pleasant activity, but it has to be done. Also some meetings are very routine affairs, and you just have to endure them, along with every one else. During such meetings, my 'doodling' becomes more and more elaborate! I just have to tell myself the end-product is worth it.

I suppose party activists are different from most people. Some people can confine their worries and interests to their own affairs, but others, the activists, feel that whatever is happening, nationally or internationally, is somehow their business. We are the interferers: we feel that everything that takes place is to some extent a part of our responsibility, and that we are called upon to take some sort of action in conequence. And while individual problems call for individual action, social problems require social solutions. So we decide to join together to determine a joint course of action. This is obviously not the response of the majority of people. Most people confine their political activity merely to voting for a certain party. Perhaps we are generally regarded as a sort of 'lunatic fringe'! As for reasons why most people avoid becoming political activists, some have no clear political convictions, while others feel embarrassed at the thought of being identified with a particular political party. Some people have work in which they feel they should avoid overt political commitment, doctors, clergymen or civil servants, perhaps — but mostly, I think, people prefer to devote their time and energy to their own personal responsibilities and interests. They do not consider that the world of politics has anything to do with them.

What do you say to the view that if we are a 'lunatic fringe' it is right that our views should not prevail?

I think that when people are very highly motivated, that motivation should be given some weight. Those who are highly motivated are likely to keep themselves better informed about the course of political events, and to be more concerned about achieving certain ends, and avoiding certain mistakes. It seems to me reasonable that their views should be given some special recognition. But at the same time I am concerned that party membership in general is declining, and that the Labour Party may cease to be a mass party. We are concerned with the well-being of ordinary people, and I think it is essential that we should attract a wide variety of members. I should like to see far more people take a part in the positive side of politics. Then it seems to me it would be wholly reasonable that party activists should be given a larger share of responsibility in guiding party destinies. There is a return on time invested in politics in terms of personal satisfaction, friendship and so on, but that return ought to include some degree of influence over the course of events, at least within the party. There must at least be the possibility of that, and certainly more so than at present.

Has your political activity influenced your children?

I think they will always be Labour supporters. They have a strong sense of justice, and I believe they associate Labour Party policies with this, in a generalised way. They understand why we are involved with the party, and take quite strong partisan attitudes on certain issues. However, they may be deterred from becoming activists themselves, as they have seen how much of my time has been taken up with political work over the past few years. They want to enjoy all the ordinary pleasures and interests of other young people of their age, and I should never try to influence them to become seriously involved when they have no deep desire to do so. Perhaps at some later stage they may decide to take a more active role.

Having made the initial decision to join the Labour Party, I shall remain as a member, and I hope as an activist. It was not an easy decision; for a long while I did not relish the compromise required in the real world of politics, and preferred to keep my ideals pure. This now seems to me to be self-indulgent.

I have had some difficult times in the Labour Party, and have found myself part of a small, unpopular minority on at least one occasion, during the time of the Conservative Housing Finance Act. I felt that to

153

refuse to implement the Act would be to tread on dangerous constitutional ground, although I heartily detested the Act itself. We might subsequently find that a Conservative Council refused to implement a Labour Government's policy, I thought, and then we should be on very weak ground. This was a time of considerable strain, but finally the whole issue subsided, and relationships were restored. I suppose divisive political issues of this kind are bound to arise from time to time, and part of the task of the political activist is to learn to outlive them.

I have no confidence that a future Labour Government will carry out policies to which the Labour Party as a whole is committed, but I shall continue to work for the Labour Party because I have no alternative. The Labour Party is the only group which has the possibility of representing the working people of this country, and establishing a more equitable and humane society.

Age 31. A 'heterosexual bachelor'.
Cambridge graduate. Buying own flat.
An economist with the Electricity
Generating Board.

My family moved to Putney in 1964 when I was 16. I was not then
particularly interested in politics. I became interested between school
and university. When I went up to Cambridge I drifted into the Young
Liberals partly because of my hostility to policies then being pursued
by Harold Wilson's Government and I continued to be active with them
on my return to Putney. I was a member of the Putney Young Liberals
when Peter Hain was Chairman. I became disenchanted with them and
was driven to more orthodox socialism when they became divided
between a right wing and pavement politics. Eventually I decided that I
had made a fool of myself by joining the Liberals and in 1972 I went
into the Putney Labour Party offices, met Ian McGarry, went to a ward
Annual General Meeting and the next thing I knew I was Ward
Membership Officer and a member of the General Management
Committee! I've never been able to get out of it since.

I found that the Putney Labour Party as a social environment was
fun to be in but, more important, there were things to be done and if
people like me did not do them they would *not* be done. Within a
year I was Secretary of the West Hill Ward, I stood, unsuccessfully, in
the 1974 Council Elections and did some organising in the first general
election of that year. At that time I probably belonged in the social-
democratic wing of the Labour Party but partly as a result of
observation and partly as a result, I suspect, of the political
environment in Putney (I don't want to overstate that and be thought
of as a political chameleon) I found myself moving to the left. After a
while it became important for me to stay in Putney rather than risk
going into some firmly social-democratic Labour Party. This came up
towards the end of 1976 when, having saved up enough money to
decide to buy myself somewhere to live, I had to decide whether to
move or not. I decided to stay in Putney.

My flat is not suitable for permanent co-habitation so if I went in
for some permanent arrangement I should have to get somewhere else
but might well stay in Putney even then. My job with the Electricity
Generating Board is fairly lucrative and I find it intellectually very, very

interesting. If you're working for a nationalised industry you are seeing some of the nuts and bolts of what socialism might be about. It teaches one that while if you take over a plastic bucket industry you haven't got socialism, on the other hand nationalised industries are *not* capitalist enterprises under another name. There are all kinds of differences in what you might call the general culture of them; for example, in nationalised industries, staff as well as manual members are unionised; that is not true in ICI or in BP. Another thing, I have never heard anybody talking in board meetings about profitability, or even all that much about increasing sales but people talk a hell of a lot about their responsibility to the consumer. Some of it may be pure rhetoric but it *is* a different culture and I think a desirable one.

I've unsuccessfully contested Council seats three times now and I've been on the Local Government Committee. I'm also active in the wider Labour movement. I sit on three committees of the Fabian Society; they published a pamphlet of mine in 1974 and I'm co-author of one coming out next year. The first one was about state holding companies — a critique of the NEB proposals — not a particularly hostile one; the next one is about energy policy.

For the last two years I've been Ward Secretary of the new ward of West Putney, I'm also Membership Officer and on the Executive Committee of the party as well as the General Committee. And I'm on the Premises Committee. If you only do one job as everything must have rough patches you could get very depressed but as all your jobs can't be troublesome at the same time you're in quite a favoured position!

When I joined the Labour Party I had a pretty strange mixture of attitudes but during the period of the last Labour Government I found myself moving further to the left. Nevertheless, I don't think central government can successfully be defied over any period and I think the Putney Party has moved a little towards my position on this. On the other hand I have moved massively towards the party's position on such matters as the EEC. At the beginning I was more or less in favour of going in. Now I think we shall almost certainly have to withdraw.

Putney Labour Party is pretty lively and well-organised. I've heard scarifying stories of local parties in other parts of the country and I know it took my sister 18 months to join her local branch. The Putney Party is not particularly cliqueish. Some people try to make it so but they're not very successful and because Putney spends a lot of the time actually doing things it preserves a degree of momentum. It's a fairly large party, a campaigning party and it has a capacity to be tolerant.

But until quite recently one was being dragged out every Sunday morning to do something or other and I can't say that I welcomed this, it tended to interfere with my social life. As for the future I'm on the local government panel of possible candidates and will hope to stand in a by-election or in the 1982 Borough Council elections. I've also put my name forward for the GLC election but I don't expect anything will come of this. As for parliamentary ambitions I take the view that one should think about this relatively late in life when you know what you're doing. I can't think of a more debilitating and useless existence than hunting around for seats, often hopeless ones, at a time when you should be either working things out for yourself or campaigning over specific issues. I think the perpetual candidate, particularly the comparatively young perpetual candidate is a menace. So far as I'm personally concerned, I might somewhere in my middle thirties decide to have a stab but in no circumstances would it be Putney. This is because the prophet is never honoured in his own country and there are always factions for and factions against any local person. Someone who comes from some distance away, other things being equal, is a safer person to have. When you got selected for Putney there was, in Labour Party terms, a quasi-revolutionary situation but under normal conditions I would not favour selecting someone from our own constituency.

I'm 31, married with two young children and I've lived in Putney since I was two years old. My husband and I joined the Labour Party together at the time of the first 1974 general election for which we did some work. I teach part-time at home under the ILEA home-tuition scheme and part-time at South Thames College. I have been on the General Management Committee of the Putney Party for several years.

I see no point in being a non-active member and joined with the full intention of being active. I enjoy some party work but I'm irritated by the endless jumble sales and bazaars which can detract from political discussion and activity. I realise it's got to be done and admire the people who do it. The Putney Labour Party seems to me to be basically united and to be remarkably free from the tensions which are said to exist in the party as a whole; there is plenty of opportunity for free discussion but also a very strong corporate feeling and a knowledge of what has to be done, of what the essential issues are. I don't think I have personally influenced decisions but that is not what I'm particularly interested in doing; I think we act as a party and not as an amalgam of individuals.

I was Branch Secretary of Thamesfield Ward for two years and have toyed with the idea of standing for the Council but it is difficult while the children are young. Perhaps I will think about it in the future. I served on the Roehampton Community Health Council for two years. Although I found the experience interesting and instructive I felt constantly irritated by the lack of any real power the CHC has to improve health services.

I read European studies at Sussex and art history at Oxford University. After an unlikeable short spell in art publishing and two enjoyable years teaching in a boys' grammar school I returned to university to do a teaching certificate. Since then I have taught full or part-time in higher education colleges. I'm therefore particularly interested in education policy and deplore the cuts made by the present government. Such cuts will have disastrous long-term consequences. My other main concern is immigration.

I'm a member of the Labour Party because I feel we need a fairer distribution of wealth and resources within society. While the voluntary sector has made a valuable contribution towards social justice, the fundamental changes in society are brought about by political means. The Labour Party needs to be tougher on the racists in its midst and not to be afraid to condemn racism for fear of losing votes.

I've a lot of interests outside politics — music, art, travel and bringing up children.

LINDSAY THOMAS

26. Graduate of Sussex University.
Went to a public school (Uppingham).

I joined the Labour Party while I was at university. My parents were anything but Labour, my father being some distance to the right of the *Daily Telegraph*. While I was at school I did a lot of hitch-hiking, round Europe, for example and, I suppose, I was a part of the youth movement of the late sixties. I hitched out to Istanbul and went from there by train to India and became deeply involved in political discussions there. I developed my socialist ideas while I was at university. While there I saw my father once a year to negotiate the grant. The discussions regularly broke down. My mother was rather liberal and by no means as hostile towards my move to the left as my father.

I came to London after university because my girl friend was working here (we have been living together for some years now) and I then spent seven months on the dole, looking for a job. Eventually I got a job through the Professional and Executive Register with KLG, my present employers, whose factory, as you know, is here in Roehampton. Before that I lived in Islington where I was also a member of the local party and joined the party here as a matter of course when we moved to Putney.

By then I'd been in three or four constituencies and was a committed Labour activist. I knew about Putney before I actually joined this party and was glad to have it confirmed when I got here that Putney was active and with a good number of younger people. What is more the Putney Party has thinkers in it, that is crucial and the party has fantastic potential – the best CLP I've ever been in.

The first meeting I attended was a social one which you held here in your flat in 1978. Peter Hain was here and I said that I never thought to see him at a Labour Party occasion (we had met in the student movement) and he said he thought I was a member of the Communist Party! Your speech that night encouraged me enormously.

This period of Tory ascendancy would be more depressing to me if I lived somewhere other than in Putney, simply because here things are developing and while this cannot overcome electoral disasters the results of my political work here and in the factory are encouraging. I am engaged in a day-to-day political struggle to win people to the party, to strengthen the trade unions and to be active and that's coming along quite well. There's a lot of ground for optimism.

At KLG I'm a Stock Controller and am the APEX Branch Secretary (Association of Professional, Executive, Clerical and Computer Staffs). We had a meeting and agreed by fourteen votes to one with one abstention, to affiliate to the Putney Labour Party and I now represent them on the Putney GMC. It is very fruitful just now to work for socialism in a factory. I am particularly interested in the link between the trade unions and the party which ought to be much better than it is at local level. The trade unions can't criticise the Labour Party while ours is the only one at KLG which meets monthly and gets attendances of 30 to 40 per cent of the membership — elsewhere it's often 1 per cent or even less.

The Putney Labour Party GMC meetings are much better than those of other parties I've attended, they're more interesting, involve more political discussion but there's still a lot of room for improvement if they're to become more effective at decision-making. The Executive Committee of the party takes decisions on matters presented to it but does not innovate and put forward plans for future action. To provide an effective leadership an Executive Committee should set objectives for the party and organise to reach them; matters such as finance and membership and other internal problems and externally we should prepare campaigns and set priorities for the next two or three years. Then we ought to be prepared to go out to organised sections of the community, to youth groups, church groups and so on and seek to discuss our ideas with them. The party never disappears but never operates at full stretch except at elections; it just keeps going (Laughs.)

Now I'm acting as Youth Officer of the party I shall be on the EC of the Putney Party and will hope to move some of these ideas there. The party really had no policy at the last general election except to say that we won't do this or we don't do that; certainly there's no policy agreement between the parliamentary leadership and Annual Conference. The Tories came in with amazing backwards reforms which they have implemented very quickly; if we had gone into the last election with positive policies we should have done better, we might have won. We had the same problem in Wandsworth where the Tories won again on the same basis. I've been to the Local Government Committee recently where I nearly fell asleep; we went through an Agenda but nothing positive emerged. I'm concentrating now on the Putney Labour Party and on my political work in the factory.

It is important that Labour's position has now gained credibility among the people with whom I work and associate in the trade union and people gradually get drawn in; the Tories now have no credibility at all and they've given up. Similarly we could also raise the presence of the party in the nearby Putney Vale Estate and could increase morale in this small community.

Soon after I joined the Labour Party at university I went to a special meeting at Lewes where a presentation was being made to an old member of the party. I thought it would be the most incredible bore but the old man gave a beautiful speech which outlined the difficulties of the early days but insisted on the hope despite all the setbacks and retreats and he still had confidence. It was very emotive and a great boost to morale. I have that confidence and hope stronger than ever, particularly since I've worked in manufacturing industry. It's not the utopia that people used to think of but a developing socialism is not only desirable it is actually necessary and that is the challenge.

The first part of this book describes the political struggle which took place in the Putney Labour Party in the early sixties. The outcome of that bitter contest revealed that the 'left' had gained ascendancy in the party; the old guard was defeated and I, a nuclear disarmer and Chairman of 'Victory for Socialism' was selected as candidate and subsequently elected to Parliament in 1964.

It was never the case, however, that the party was 'taken over' by a collection of hard-line socialists dedicated to a Marxist line of policy. I doubt whether more than half a dozen members of the party have read any Marx and only a small minority buy and read the *Morning Star* or the other periodicals of the various factions who inhabit the left of the party. This became clear in the second part of the book in which members of the Putney Party spoke for themselves. Here are no closed minds, no fanatical activists, yet these are the people who, for the most part, believe that their role as working party members means that they should have a say in framing party policy. What is more, most of them believe they are entitled to require the party in Parliament to carry out the policies determined by the party at Annual Conference; they think that their MP should be subject to re-selection and replacement if they so decide and also hold the view that the party leader should be selected by a wider and more representative body than the parliamentary Labour Party. These views are held, not by a way-out band of hard-liners but by a cross-section of the people who enable the Labour Party to function effectively in Putney.

I have been fortunate in my comrades in the Putney Labour Party. In the preceding section of this book there is to be found selflessness and idealism, qualities remote from the pen of the hard-boiled political journalist and yet, I do believe, also present in other Labour parties throughout the country as they are here in Putney. As one narrative has succeeded another, the story of Labour in Putney has unfolded before our eyes but it is now necessary to remind the reader of some of the salient features of the 15-year period in which I represented the constituency in Parliament and to summarise the interviews.

The reader will have spotted that the Putney constituency has changed a good deal since the war. Until I was first elected in 1964 it was always regarded as a safe Tory seat. What changed all this? First it was the putting forward of a clear socialist message to the voter.

163

After my adoption as candidate, we all determined that the electorate would not be confused as to what I stood for. There was to be no pussy-foot looking for the middle ground, wherever that might be. After all had not Dick Taverne fought the constituency in 1959 on a middle of the road ticket and achieved nothing?

Secondly, as I think comes over strongly in the interviews, although the Campaign for Nuclear Disarmament caused some internal dissension, it also stimulated political discussion within the party. Even the imposition of an NEC enquiry had its beneficial side effects. What helped most to heal the wounds after the enquiry, was that the ordinary party workers felt that the intervention of the party hierarchy had been heavy-handed and ill-informed. Under hostile pressure there is a tremendous impetus to forget old scores and pull together. But that is not all. CND brought into the party a group of articulate socialists who, to start with, may have come in for the political debate but who stayed on to become loyal and dedicated workers for the cause. The party never became boring again. I am sure that in all successful constituency Labour parties there is a maximum of lively political debate. It is a commonplace that for a party to survive it must put fund-raising at the top of its priorities for action. I do not dispute that In my time I have spent my fair share at bazaars, fairs and so on. Indeed in Putney I would say that those events were sometimes brilliantly organised. The point is that unless there is political debate, new members do not join the party or if they do they quickly become disillusioned. If the party does not attract new members, the old members, who are only mortal, become more and more resentful at having to do more and more of the work. In the Labour Party it is too easy to regard the fund-raising activities as the end and not the means. This was never the case in Putney.

It is alleged that those who say most do the least work. On the basis of the Putney Party this was generally untrue. Some of the keenest workers in Putney were also excellent debaters and several became leading members of the Borough Council. I often wondered how some of them found the time to do so many things well.

Phyllis Courtney, who was once described to me as the epitome of the Putney Labour Party, said in her interview that although a lot of marriages within the party had broken up this might be no more than the national average. Perhaps a sociologist will give us the answer but few would deny that active politics does place a strain on personal relationships. Generally, husbands and wives in the Putney Party appeared to agree closely on most political issues. This was just as well as continuous disagreement with your partner on a major political issue could well bring about a permanent rift. I hasten to say that I speak from the security of over 40 years of happy marriage. There have been and still are disagreements and differences of emphasis but these are overridden in the case of Marie and myself by the broad similarity of our general approach to politics.

An important factor which indisputably worked in our favour in Putney was demographic change. As Elizabeth Mitchell said in her interview, after the war when she moved to Roehampton, the Manresa Jesuits still ran a farm on what is now the vast GLC Alton Estate. Sam Dougherty stresses just how great an improvement these estates were over the slums in which many of my interviewees grew up. Many like him are puzzled at the way in which high-rise developments have become the focus for vandalism. This is still less of a problem in Roehampton and Putney than is the case elsewhere. Indeed, my wife and I, working among the estates for many years, have previously found the majority of the tenants very happy with their accommodation. More recent national and local government policies have dispelled much of this content. Appalling maintenance and swingeing rent increases have brought home more clearly than any politician could, the penalties for ordinary people living under a Conservative administration whether in the Town Hall or at Westminster. After regaining control over the Borough Council in 1978, one of the meanest and most pointless things the Tories did was to remove the two tenants' representatives from the Housing Committee. Participation by all parties had previously been sought after. It is now clear that the Tories want to impose their will regardless of the views of their tenants.

No account of the recent history of the Putney Labour Party would be complete without once again stressing the value of Ian McGarry to the fortunes of the party. In 1964, when Ian became Secretary/Agent of the party, things seemed to be in poor shape. The NEC enquiry had just taken place and it was a commonly held view that my candidature would ensure yet another Conservative win at the next general election. So-called moderates regarded this as the most telling argument against my adoption as candidate. It may be a political cliché that organisation wins elections but it is not entirely true. Nevertheless, it is safe to say that without Ian's inspiration and management skills we would never have won Putney. Perhaps this is the secret of it. Although Ian is a brilliant organiser, he is an even better politician. I have rarely met anyone who was better able to balance faction against faction; personality against personality. He welded the party together again after the traumas of the NEC enquiry and kept it together for almost all of the 15 years I represented the constituency in Parliament. From 1971 to 1977, he showed remarkable gifts as leader of the controlling Labour Group on the Wandsworth Borough Council. His greatest achievement was to hold the group together in 1971 in the face of the Conservative Housing Finance Act which imposed across the board rent increases. He was, in the jargon of those days, a 'non-implementer'. In other words he was in favour of not implementing what he regarded as class-biased legislation aimed at council tenants. He could not carry the group with him and so resigned as leader of the council along with a significant number of committee chairmen. Within six months he was back as leader and the group took up where it had left off.

In his role as Secretary of the Putney constituency Labour Party, McGarry was involved in another unpleasant aspect of the Housing Finance Act. Putney CLP, unlike Battersea and Tooting CLPs, the other constituents of the London Borough of Wandsworth, had passed a resolution in its GMC instructing all Putney Councillors regardless of whether they represented Putney wards on the Borough Council, to vote in the group against implementation. The group, as noted, by a narrow majority voted for implementation. The Putney GMC took a dim view of those Councillors who had voted for implementation and contemplated having them expelled from the party. As Ian McGarry must have realised, such a move if it had come to pass, would not just have been embarassing politically; it would almost certainly have invited yet another NEC investigation. Amazingly, Ian managed to head off this confrontation and although the Councillors had to appear to answer the charges against them at a special meeting of the GMC, the expulsion resolution was lost. In spite of this difficult interlude, Ian managed to pull the party round in very little time. Once again, in spite of losing the overwhelmingly Labour ward of Fairfields to Battersea South because of Boundary redistribution, against the odds, we won Putney for Labour in 1974. There is a slight moral to this tale. One of the Councillors who had so stoutly defended himself for his support of implementation, within a year had left the constituency and joined the Conservative Party. It is difficult for a non-socialist to be a member of the Labour Party.

The history of any constituency Labour Party over a number of years is bound to be one of failure and success. I was fortunate that during my long association as MP with the Putney Party, success always outbalanced failure. The parliamentary seat was held until the disappointment of 1979; the Borough Council was only lost twice, in 1968/71 and again in 1978; my wife Marie held the GLC seat until 1977. These were good times from an election-winning point of view.

It is remarkable that some of these successes, particularly the winning of the parliamentary seat, were achieved at times when nearly every expert predicted that we should lose. My opinions on political commentators may be inferred from reading this book and I will not expand on them here; but I still believe that the magic ingredient in our success notwithstanding superb organisation without which nothing would have been possible, was the uncompromising and clear message of socialism that we put over both within the party and to the electorate. I have been flattered by the number of interviews which have made the point that at no time did the ordinary party member feel that his views were being ignored by the MP. Accountability will be strengthened in the Labour Party if the proposals on automatic re-selection of MPs are properly carried out. In the Putney Party, this procedure would, I am sure, have made no change in candidature. I always tried to take full account of what the party felt was its grass roots, sometimes to the aggravation of parliamentary colleagues. I am glad that this way of doing things was appreciated by the membership. Really, it is so much nonsense to believe that things can properly be otherwise. I find the patronising attitude of some MPs towards those who put them into Parliament quite sickening. Indeed, I am sure this attitude plus hastily assembled consensus policies, ensured a rough ride for Labour in power and contributed to ignominious defeats such as that of 1979.

At the beginning I quoted Winston Churchill's saying, 'We are, more than we know, the creatures of our institutions.' Labour representatives are often caught in this trap and keen young socialists finish up by being mere Councillors or parliamentarians; the institution has taken over. This is the main and unrecognised cause of the gap which has so often grown up between the rank and file of our party and its representatives at the Town Hall or in Parliament. It is easier, because it is closer, for the party to keep its influence to the fore in the municipality than at Westminster where distance and tradition combine to reduce the power of the party to nullity. This is particularly the case when Labour is in office. In opposition, the party machine is quite closely involved but in office the links are deliberately broken; the Cabinet is appointed by the Prime Minister instead of being elected by the party as is the Shadow Cabinet; the Whips Office moves into Downing Street and party influence is demoted; the party is expelled from government and reduced to the level of the occasional attendance of the Secretary at meetings of the parliamentary Labour Party which are informal gatherings at which members are allowed to conceal the way they vote from their own constituency parties. Thus the idea of the parliamentary party as an organisation of its own, separate from the rest of the party and having its own ethos and independent views has grown up. It is a thoroughly disruptive and undemocratic notion and the cause of much trouble. It should come to an end and the parliamentary Labour Party should be brought within the orbit of those who by their work and trust bring about its membership.

Another difficulty which rank and file members of the Labour Party have had to contend with in recent years has been the growth of the habit of regarding political parties as having common motivations. Political commentators and pollsters work on this assumption, quite regardless of the fact that what drives a Tory voter repels a socialist and vice versa, which is why they are so often wrong. These assumptions inform the leader columns of the newspapers and it is quite firmly believed that any bold statement of socialist principle will be a vote loser. My experience is to the contrary. I believe that one should actively seek to offend the opposition and that only by doing so will one retain the enthusiastic support of one's own people. The Tories in Putney always went out of their way to paint me as an extremist and I think that nothing helped more than that to keep the Putney Party in good shape. Elections are not lost by Tories voting against you but by the failure of your own people to turn out. If the party is in good heart they will get your vote out. In the end our own leadership made it impossible for us to hold the seat. We might have won in October 1978 but the winter of discontent took the heart out of our troops and although we made a brave effort it was not enough to defeat the ebullient Tories whose morale was higher than ours.

A main purpose of this book has been to show what ordinary members of a constituency Labour Party feel; what made them join the party in the first place; what keeps them politically active, and to some extent what effect political awareness has had on their private lives. Inevitably, as the interviews were deliberately unstuctured, no clear picture comes across. I am relieved about this because it would depress me mightily if I thought all members of the party came out of the same pod. I sometimes have this feeling about the Conservative Party — that it is uniform because it is not interested in ideology; but rather in the preservation of class privileges and rights over property. Why do people join the Labour Party? The evidence of these interviews is that although Messrs Butler and Stokes will be reassured by the number of members who come from good Labour voting backgrounds, nearly as many come from quite different homes. Some of these could be described as middle class in the usual language of our society. Some of them are resented if only mildly by the more traditional members of the party. But why did they join? For a few, it was a question of wanting to get into politics at a local level and deliberately choosing the Labour Party after looking at the alternatives. Although few mentioned the Conservatives as a possible outlet at an earlier stage for their political activity, some favoured the Liberal Party. Peter Hain, as is well known, came to the Labour Party after a long spell with the Liberals; indeed, at one time he had been a member of their national executive. But others too had been at one time Liberals. There is sometimes a conscious process of selection which goes on before a party is chosen in which to be politically active. Strangely, the prior contemplation of an alternative does not seem to influence the choice of ideological views once the plunge has been taken and the Labour Party joined. As many former Liberal-inclined members move to the left as to the right. But the larger element in this middle-class group of members joined the party from a deeply felt conviction, usually formed at an early age, that socialism was morally correct. Some of these may have come from a Christian background and discovered that the only form of practical Christianity possible today is to work for socialism. Most of these members, but not all, end up as socialists rather than social democrats. Once the party has been joined another important aspect of membership is camaraderie. It would be wrong to give the impression that the Labour Party is solely an organisation which gives support to lonely people. On the other hand it does bring great comfort very often to a number of shy people living on their own to whom it represents their main point of contact with the world outside. The media will naturally be interested in those members of the party who arrive via the Communist Party or other revolutionary groupings of the far left. This book will disappoint them. Several members of the party have come from the CP; but I am sure they will forgive me if I describe them as being now in the centre of the Labour Party — hardly voracious moles chewing the fabric of our society. One of my interviewees certainly could be described as a Trotskyist. Unfortunately, she has moved from the constituency. She was never a party officer or a local councillor let alone a parliamentary candidate. But she was a dedicated party worker and as such is sorely missed.

A constant theme of this book has been that to keep members active both politically and for the more mundane purposes of collecting subscriptions and running jumble sales, a constituency party must put socialist politics first. A slightly disturbing theme has from time to time cropped up in the interviews that the Putney Party is slowly running down the discussion of politics. Happily, it is a trend which the majority claimed had been halted. It seems to me common sense that whenever political discussion takes place there is bound to be a move in the direction of socialism. The fashionable analysis is that the smaller the party membership the more likely the party is to be subverted by the far left. In my view the opposite is true. A small clique in control of a party is much more likely to be dedicated to the preservation of ossified right-wing views hopelessly out of tune with the aspiration or interests of the electorate. A big party is almost certain to take socialist attitudes to affairs national and local. The majority in a big party is influenced by the thoughts and actions of a smaller group who will set the intellectual analysis of events. This majority will normally be intensely loyal to the highly active group which gives the party its officers and its council candidates. They remain loyal because for them there is no ambition to become anything other than rank and file members. They are not open to patronage. Within the small elite group at the top of the party this does not hold true. In Putney as elsewhere, there are occasional outbreaks of back-stabbing and general unpleasantness. But here it is not necessary to have far left opinions to be a member of the elite group. There is an uncanny recognition of real calibre among ordinary party members which transcends political views. It would on the other hand be remarkable if a party officer or local government candidate were selected who did not, in the view of the rank and file members, pull his weight in jumble sales and routine party work.

But what are the major political preoccupations of the Putney Party? It would appear from the interviews that they are local rather than national or international. This may be rather misleading. A great many of my interviewees had been or were local Councillors and so it was natural that local affairs should dominate their minds. Nearly everyone was fed up with the debate on party organisation. All the interviewees regarded the justness of the case for automatic re-selection of MPs; for a broader college to elect future leaders and for the NEC to have control over the writing of the party's election manifesto, as proved beyond the need for further debate. Again the continuing membership of the European Economic Community by the United Kingdom, the one international issue that came to the fore, was considered disastrous by both right and left in nearly every case. The rank and file were often forced to express their feelings of alienation from the parliamentary leadership. Without doubt, attention must be paid to this problem. In the end it is surely better to have a healthy party organisation at the constituency level than to appease a group of MPs out of touch with their supporters?

This book is dedicated to the folk of Putney; but I hope that other members of other constituency parties when they read it will recognise the animal if not the precise breed. I believe that what the members have said in these interviews is of tremendous importance to the future of the Labour Party. On its own, of course, it proves nothing, although it might suggest, in all humility, that consensus politics are made in university common rooms and Parliament and not in the real life outside.

I had my own priorities in the House of Commons. I spent much more time on the arts in general and the theatre in particular than the Putney Labour Party which, however, knowing of my connection with Actors' Equity was benevolently disposed towards my predilection. I reported regularly to the Putney General Management Committee and also held public Report Back meetings. At no time did the party try to tell me what to do in Parliament. There were differences of view from time to time but the generally left-wing approach to politics which brought about my selection as candidate remained to unite the party and myself throughout the 15 years in which I represented them and the constituency in Parliament.

An MP has to balance several loyalties which may sometimes conflict. First, he must consider the constituency party which selected him and second, the constituents who elected him. He must think of his election address and will do well to keep a copy on his desk. But he should also think of the manifesto on which his party fought the election and of the views of the Annual Conference of his party. I speak, of course, of the loyalties of a Labour Member, the annual jamboree of the Conservative Party can hardly expect to be treated as a serious policy-making body. Next, a Labour Member must consider the views of the parliamentary Labour Party and, when in office, of his government as expressed through the Whips. I put the Whips last. They are there, not to tell you what to do but to encourage you to be present on important occasions and to indicate the government's wishes. For the most part they will be identical with the desires of the Member but every now and then a crisis of conscience will arise and a member will find his loyalties pulling in different directions. When that occurs, he can only follow the advice of old Polonius:

This above all,-To thine own self be true
And it must follow, as the night the day,
Thou canst not then be false to any man.

From the beginning I was extremely active in the House, as may
be seen from the extract of the Hansard Index printed here as an
Appendix, and from the beginning we held an advice 'surgery' on
most Friday evenings throughout the year. My wife was usually there
as the Greater London Councillor and we often had a Borough
Councillor as well and so were able to give informed help at any level
of government. We also kept up regular contributions and
correspondence in the local newspapers.

There was never any doubt about my own position. Even before
the 1966 general election I had supported a motion criticising the
Labour Government for backing the American resumption of bombing
in Vietnam and I had joined the 'Tribune' group as a matter of course
At the general election of 1966 I called for a re-statement of socialist
aims in terms containing 'the basic emotional and intellectual food
which has nourished every worthwhile movement in the history of
mankind' and I claimed that our sources included John Wesley and
Karl Marx, taking in Hyndman, Hardie, Robert Owen, William Morris
and the Fabians on the way. 'That is why the Labour Party has a
collection of beliefs rather than a single dogma. We still have those
beliefs. We must never lose them. We must never degenerate into a
mere electoral machine.'

At the election which followed my majority was more than
doubled.

In the years that followed I balanced my left-wing activities with
efforts on matters of constituency importance. I was able to mitigate
aircraft noise in Putney by securing changes in the approach to
Heathrow but I also maintained opposition to Polaris submarines by
abstaining, with others, on the defence vote. When all the parties
encouraged their members to support Britain's application to join the
Common Market by imposing, in effect, a nine-line Whip, I voted
in the 'No' lobby with a handful of others. This action received
support in the *Wandsworth Borough News* as did my refusal of
support when the government deprived the surgical limb-fitters at
Roehampton of a negotiated increase in wages.

Throughout my time in Parliament I kept up the struggle
against aircraft noise, opposing Concorde, taking a complaint to the
Ombudsman and so on. Even before I was an MP, on the London
County Council and elsewhere I had campaigned against the farcical

pretence of civil defence against nuclear war. In 1968 the Labour Government decided to disband the Civil Defence Corps and my only complaint was that they did not follow it up by abandoning the British nuclear weapon. I put down a motion on the Order Paper.

> This House, recognising the truth of the statements made to the House from both front benches that this country could not survive a nuclear war, congratulates the Government on its decision to disband the Civil Defence Corps and the Auxiliary Fire Service and urges that the logic of these decisions is to close down the Polaris base and denuclearise British defence.

Later in that year I abstained on the government's Immigration Bill. I supported the proposal to televise our proceedings and tried, again unsuccessfully, to introduce a Bill to control aircraft noise.

At that time the Labour Government was low in public esteem and talking to the Putney Party I urged them to struggle on, 'Maintaining confidence in each other and recognising that if the Government can be persuaded to keep faith with its own principles it can still recover.'

At this time a proposed code of conduct for members was being debated in the parliamentary Labour Party. I made it clear that I could not agree to be bound by a code which sought to place the parliamentary party above both the constituency parties and Annual Conference and suggested an additional clause providing that no member could be penalised for acting in accordance with Conference decisions or election manifesto pledges.

At a conference in London I urged the government to take greater account of constituency opinion, arguing that the government's loss of popularity was largely due to their failure to keep in step with their own supporters.

At that time there were still a few people living in Putney in wartime prefabricated houses which were, by then, qute unfit for human habitation. By creating a considerable public fuss I was able to get all the remaining tenants moved into reasonable accommodation in a surprisingly short time.

In 1969 I voted against my own government again, this time on proposals to increase charges for dentures and spectacles and in this year I spent much time in public correspondence with London Transport trying to improve the bus and Underground services in the constituency.

In a speech to the Methodist Synod, held that year at Southlands

College in Putney, I said that I inhabited a kind of no man's land which existed between unitarianism, humanism and agnosticism and added: 'As a natural dissenter myself I have an interest in seeing that the flame of dissent is kept burning bright in every area of human activity!'

The following year we regained the Greater London Council, Marie topping the local poll and later in 1970 I urged that negotiations on the Common Market should not begin so that we might avoid 'the possibility of suffering the grave misfortune of a successful outcome'.

I voted against my own government once again on Vietnam and Cambodia and addressed a meeting in Trafalgar Square. A march to the American Embassy in Grosvenor Square then took place where some disorder occurred with regrettable injuries both among demonstrators and in the police who were badly deployed on this occasion. A confrontation of this sort must occasionally occur in a free society and when it does I am always torn in my sympathies which extend both to the demonstrators and to the police. I was unable to sustain this duality when I was once pushed down a basement by the rump of a policeman's horse!

One of my numerous failures was my attempt in 1970 to persuade London Transport to extend the Underground to Roehampton instead of building the Heathrow extension.

Labour lost the 1970 general election but we held on to Putney in a campaign started by Harold Wilson. Mary Wilson was hit by a bag of flour and a photographer collected an egg intended for Harold. This was, perhaps, the most remarkable result of my 15 years as a Member. To gain Putney in 1964 was surprising; to hold it in the Tory victory of 1970 was astonishing, a great victory for the Putney Labour Party, for every man and woman in it worked in that election with an irresistible enthusiasm, evidence of which may be seen in the contributions which make up the main part of this book.

Early in the following year St Mary's Parish Church saw its most important meeting since 1647 when a tremendous all-party campaign opened against the motorway which was planned to carve Putney apart. Seven hundred people came to protest and as this was matched elsewhere in London, the proposed Ringway 2 was quietly buried and has never surfaced since. The whole operation, in which Douglas Jay, the Labour Member for Battersea played a leading part, demonstrated that the public *can* prevail if they choose to exert themselves.

For a good part of my time as Member of Parliament for Putney, my wife represented the constituency on the Greater London Council and every week the local papers reported questions from one or the other of us on local issues. In the House I continued to vote and speak

174

against entry into the Common Market and kept up the battle against aircraft noise.

Early in 1972 a joint campaign against the government's Housing Finance Bill took place with tenants' associations, GLC and Wandsworth Borough Council representatives combining together in total opposition to the measure which was being opposed most vigorously in the House of Commons. Later in the year I carried a motion by a narrow majority at the Putney Literary and Debating Society. It was 'That pressure groups and parties are essential to parliamentary democracy.'

In January 1973 George Wyver died at the age of 96, remaining a fervent socialist and member of the Labour Party from its foundation to the end of his days. In the local paper I said:

> It was and still is a source of pride to me that I was the means whereby one of his chief ambitions, to see Putney with a Labour MP was realised while he was still able to enjoy it to the full and to see it for what it was — the end product of years of missionary work and of sheer hard, unremitting and unrewarded effort.

Later that year Marie easily held her seat on the Greater London Council but the Boundary Commission then removed the safe Labour Fairfield Ward from Putney and we went into the February 1974 general election knowing that mathematically we were likely to lose. In the event we hung on to the seat with a majority of 1,449 which we increased in the second 1974 general election in October. After February I was appointed Arts Minister by Harold Wilson and have written about this elsewhere in my book, *The Culture Gap*.

In 1975 Putney Labour Party came out strongly against staying in the Common Market and I voted against the re-negotiated terms in the House. When it came to the referendum, however, it proved impossible to generate much interest either in the Putney Labour Party or in the constituency and so the fateful decision to stay in was taken against a background of apathy.

In August 1975 a speech of mine gained widespread publicity. In it I advocated that Cabinets should be elected by MPs rather than chosen by Prime Ministers. This was taken as a personal criticism of Harold Wilson but as I was myself among his appointees this could hardly have been the case.

Later that year I was given an assurance that Putney Hospital would not be closed. Alas, four years later, when the Tories came in, they immediately changed the decision and the Hospital was closed.

I maintained my view that the active member of the party rank and file should have a greater say in affairs, and was strongly supported by the Putney Labour Party. Early in the following year Marie decided not to stand for the GLC again in 1977, after nearly 30 years in local government. We were heavily defeated at the ensuing GLC election.

In April 1976 Harold Wilson was succeeded as Prime Minister by Jim Callaghan and I was among the ministers replaced by new faces. At 68 I was not surprised to go but was certainly astonished to be asked to make way for an older man. My successor, Lord Donaldson, was 69!

In return for loss of office I secured greater freedom to talk and I spoke to the Putney Party about excessive secrecy in government and the desirability of greater disclosure of all but essentially confidential transactions. At the same time Ian McGarry was appointed Assistant General Secretary of Equity, a position which I held my self for 14 years before becoming MP for Putney in 1964. There was no member of the Putney Labour Party who was not sorry to lose Ian whose contribution to gaining and holding the seat for Labour could not be overstressed. Most of us realised that in keeping McGarry in Putney we were holding a man in a job well below his capacity and so he went with our regret but our good wishes. These were not realised in one respect for within a few years the McGarry marriage was among the many to come apart. Would it have happened had Ian stayed in Putney? Who can tell.

In 1976 Marie and I celebrated our Ruby Wedding (40 years) with a party at the House and in the same year I was made an Honorary Life Member of Equity, a rare distinction which I value. In a speech at this time I talked about myth and reality in politics saying that it was easier to believe in myth than in reality. Among the myths was the belief that our public expenditure and taxation was higher than in most European countries. I was able to show that this was by no means the case but, of course the myth was believed and it probably cost us the 1979 general election.

Throughout this period I fought a losing campaign to cancel the special rate which is imposed on all those living within three miles of Wimbledon and Putney Commons. It proved impossible to generate enough local enthusiasm to overcome the feeling in the Putney Society and elsewhere that the cancellation of the special rate might have deleterious effects upon the Commons themselves. And so the special rate, which is now becoming quite onerous, remains.

I continued to play an active part in the House and to pursue my various hobby horses throughout the seventies. One of my last speeches in the Chamber in February 1979 was an attempt to persuade the government to include children damaged by hormone pregnancy testing in a Bill to provide compensation for children suffering from vaccine damage. This on behalf of a constituent, a member of the Putney Labour Party who had endured the tragedy of a damaged child.

So we entered into the period of the 1979 general election. In common with most other people I had fully expected the election in the Autumn of 1978 but Jim Callaghan decided not to go until he was forced to do so by the Opposition's victory in their censure motion of 28 March 1979. The government was defeated by a single vote, 311 to 310 and Prime Minister Callaghan immediately announced that there would be a general election. This time the swing against Labour was too great for Putney to resist. Our vote held up very well at 20,410 but the Liberal vote declined while the Tories pulled out no less than 23,040, giving them a majority of 2,630. Thus the Tories won back the seat we had held for 15 years and Putney formed part of the substantial Conservative majority in the new House of Commons.

The Putney Party was splendid in defeat. We had arranged a party before the election, hoping against hope that we might have a victory to celebrate. Instead, everyone turned up for a rather magnificent wake. Of course, I was asked to make a speech and in it said this :

When Marie and I came to Putney we were impressed with the people who made up the Putney Labour Party and felt it would be an enjoyable experience to work in the cause with them.

So it proved and we had great victories and wonderful times. The people who form the Putney Labour Party have changed a good deal over the years though there are stalwarts such as Christine and Ian McGarry, Phyllis and Peter Courtney, Sid Gowlett and others who have been active throughout the period. But what has not changed has been the idealistic ethos of the Party.

The Putney Party consists of socialists, of people who seek to change the world away from money-grubbing and profit-seeking; who may argue about ways and means and about pace but are united in their basic purposes.

If in Parliament we had been less bowed down by the changing economic fortunes of our time, less dedicated to material advancement, the Government might have been re-elected. As it was, we tried to fight the Tories on their own level and, stooping below our best, we lost.

I am not, however, pessimistic. I believe the Conservatives will make a botch of things and that we shall return, renewed and refreshed, to resume the onward march towards a fairer, more just, less angry society than the transitional state we now inhabit.

Although I shall not be standing as your Parliamentary Candidate again, Marie and I will be staying in Putney and as ordinary members of the Party will help to keep the Red Flag flying here.

On Polling Day I visited a home for the blind in Roehampton. There I met an old lady of 90. She told me how all her life she had worked for the Labour Party, canvassing, addressing envelopes, attending meetings. 'And now,' she said 'since I can do nothing more for the Party I want you to take this for the funds and don't refuse me.'

She held out her hand, I put mine into it and received this five-pound note for the Party.

It is in the knowledge that this spirit must eventually triumph that I say my farewells as your Member of Parliament.

Are there any general lessons to be drawn from the Putney experience? I believe that the seat might have been won in 1966 and possibly in 1974 with a normal campaign. I do not believe that it could have been gained in 1964 and held in 1970 without the special ingredients which a combination of circumstances enabled us to bring to the occasions. In sum, I think we did rather better than average in Putney and, as I have said, this was achieved in part by the avoidance of the 'safe' middle ground which is, in reality, a quagmire. The belief that this middle ground is inhabited by the middle classes waiting to be won by a non-socialist Labour message has no foundation in reality. Political action stems from political conviction which, in turn, is generated by the dialectic of political discussion. We under-estimate the effect of the opinion-former in his or her own community and over-estimate that of the media and of the political leader speaking at national level on television and radio. An appeal made over the head of the activist, direct to the electorate, is an appeal which gets ignored.

The uncomfortable fact is that modern elections tend to be won or lost not so much by how people vote but by how many fail to vote. This, in turn, is largely determined by the state of morale in the party and the winner is usually the party which polls the highest proportion of its natural supporters. The tendency of Labour Party leaders to disappoint their own rank and file is therefore damaging to the party's electoral chances.

178

All this is obvious to people in marginal constituencies but political parties are not run by such people and the top echelons in Parliament are filled by Members whose occupancy of safe seats shields them from electoral truths.

The object of this book is to rescue the rank and file of one party from anonymity by presenting them to the reader as they see themselves. If I am asked how I see them, I would say they are the salt of the earth.

APPENDIX: RECORD OF HUGH JENKINS' CONTRIBUTIONS IN THE CHAMBER, 1964-5

Atlantic Nuclear Force, [711] 623.
Aviation, Ministry of:
  B.E.A. internal services, jet
    aircraft, [718] *227*.
Basutoland, elections, [716] 760.
British Guiana:
  Constitution, [706] 537.
  Detained persons, [708] *315*.
Business of the House, [706] 553,
    562; [707] 1532; [708]
    1485; [709] 1855-6; [712]
    1669; [713] 843; [717]
    692-3.
Congo, [707] *12*.
Criminals, Press articles, [714] 1941.
Defence, Ministry of:
  Bases, Cyprus, personnel, [710]
    16.
  F111A aircraft, [718] 151.
  Gurkha Brigade, [710] 22.
  Valiant aircraft, [706] 836.
Education and Science:
  Arts, The, Local Authority
    powers, [715] *317-18*.
  Boys' Club, Roehampton, [710]
    210.
  Entertainment, employment of
    children, [712] *102*.
  Wandsworth Comprehensive
    School, [705] *134*.
Employment:
  International Labour
    Organisation, Convention No.
    96, [705] *205, 206*.
  Offices, Shops and Railway
    Premises Act 1963, [706]
    162.
  Pension rights, transferability,
    [709] *20*.
Employment Agencies (Regulation)
  Bill, Presented and IR*, [716]
  496-9.
Germany, reparations, [707] 912.
Heathrow Airport, night jet flights,
  [704] 569.
Home Department:
  Civil Defence Corps, [705]
    279-80; [715] *283*.

Home Department—*cont.*
  Civil Defence Organisation,
    review, [718] 1215.
  Firearms, [705] *108*.
  International Labour Organisation
    Convention No. 96, [705]
    219-20.
  Racialist pornography, [706]
    263.
Housing:
  Building materials, stone, [703]
    93.
  Local Authority mortgages,
    [705] *253*.
  Mortgage relief and subsidies,
    cost, [715] *193*.
Labour, Ministry of:
  Employment exchanges, [710]
    932.
Local Government:
  Putney and Wandsworth High
    Streets, comprehensive
    redevelopment, [703] *28*.
  Theatres, accommodation for
    wheelchairs, [709] *193-4*.
  Theatres, Use Classes Order,
    [704] *52*.
National Finance:
  Local Government finance, [708]
    225.
  Public Service pensions: [717]
    1250-1.
    Review, [716] *124*.
Nigeria, Dr. V. Allen, [703] 221.
Nuclear tests, [714] 887.
Nuclear weapons, [714] 1464:
  [717] 223.
Prime Minister, Paris visit, [710]
  236.
Public Building and Works:
  Alton Estates, Roehampton,
    Richmond Park, [704] 853.
Railways:
  Northern Line, extension, [717]
    252.
Roads:
  Incorporated Society of
    Architects and Surveyors,